英文精読教室

第2巻

他人になってみる

柴田元幸 編・訳・註

研究社

英文精読教室
第 2 巻
他人になってみる

PRINTED IN JAPAN

はじめに

　この「英文精読教室」は、読者が英語の小説を原文で読むのを助けるためのシリーズです。

　まずは編者がこれまで読んだり訳したりしてきたなかで、とりわけ面白いと思った短篇小説を選び、6巻それぞれ、ひとつのテーマに沿って作品を並べてあります。第1巻から順に読む必要はありません。ご自分が惹かれるテーマから手にとっていただければと思います。各巻、まずはウォームアップ的にごく短い作品を据えたあとは、時代順に並んでいますが、これも順番に読む必要はありません。各作品の難易度を1～3で示してありますから（1が一番易しい）、読む際の目安にしてください。

　どの作品にも詳しい註を施しました。註というものはつねに諸刃の剣であり、読者によって「小さな親切」にも「大きなお世話」にもなりえますが、このシリーズではどちらかというと、一部の読者には「大きなお世話」になる危険も覚悟で、やや多めに註が施してあります。ご自分の読みが妥当かどうかを確認してもらえるよう、右側のページには対訳を盛り込みました。少し語学的に敷居が高い、と思える作品に関しては、まず対訳を読んでもらってから原文に向かう、というやり方もあると思います。

　「まっとうな翻訳があるなら、何も原文で読む必要はないじゃないか」とおっしゃる読者もいらっしゃるでしょう。むしろその方が多数派かもしれません。僕自身、まっとうな翻訳を作ることを、長年主たる仕事にしてきましたから、そういう読者が大勢いてくださるのはとても嬉しいことです。

その反面、原文で読むことの楽しさを味わいたい、と思われる読者も一定数おられるという確信も僕にはあります。そのなかで、何の助けもなしに辞書だけで原書を読むのはちょっと厳しい、という読者がまた一定数おられるという確信もまたあります。

　かつては近所の書店に行けば、註釈つきの英語読本や英和対訳本が並んでいて、僕も中学のころから日本のおとぎ話やO・ヘンリーの短篇などを易しい英語で書き直した本を買ってノートに訳文を書いて楽しんだものですが、ふと気がつくとそういう本もずいぶん減ってしまいました。この残念な欠如を、本シリーズが少しでも是正できれば幸いです。

編訳註者

英文精読教室
第 2 巻
他人になってみる

目次

FARWELL
Stuart Dybek

ファーウェル
スチュアート・ダイベック

難易度 1
★ ☆ ☆

スチュアート・ダイベック
（Stuart Dybek, 1942- ）

　シカゴ生まれ、シカゴ育ちの作家。旧世界の雰囲気を残した戦後シカゴの街を、独特の叙情を添えて描く。これまで発表した作品は短篇集5冊、詩集2冊と決して多くないが、作家をはじめとする多くの文学愛好者の敬意を得ている。ここに収めた "Farwell" は、シカゴの街を多面的に描いた連作短篇集（a novel-in-stories）の要素が強い第2短篇集 *The Coast of Chicago*（1990）の巻頭に収められている。

Tonight, a ❶steady drizzle, streetlights ❷smoldering in fog ❸like funnels of light collecting rain. Down Farwell, the balcony windows of the apartment building where my friend Babovitch once lived, ❹reflected across the wet tennis courts, ❺and

5 I wondered if I would ever leave this city. I remembered the first night I walked down Farwell to visit Babo. He was teaching a class in Russian literature that I was taking, and had ❻invited me over. ❼I'd never had a teacher invite me to his home before. "When's a good time?" I asked.

10 ❽"I can *always* use the company," he answered, ❾scrawling out his address. "There's no phone."

It was a winter night, snowing. His apartment building was ❿the last one on the block where the street ⓫dead-ended against the lake. Behind ⓬a snow-clotted cyclone fence, the tennis courts

15 were ⓭drifted over, and beyond the courts and a small, lakeside park, a white ⓮pier extended to a green ⓯beacon. Snow had

---

❶ steady drizzle: 間断なく降る霧雨
❷ smolder(ing): くすぶる
❸ like funnels of light collecting rain: funnel(s) は「じょうご」で、街灯の光に淡く照らし出される雨を比喩的に描いた表現。
❹ reflect(ed): 映し出される、映っている。across the wet tennis courts と続くので、テニスコート一面に、明かりの灯った窓が並んで映っている感じ。
❺ and I wondered if I would ever leave this city: テニスコートに並んで映る窓を見て、「自分はいつかこの街を去るんだろうか」と考える、というのは明らかに飛躍がある。そのあいだには、最後まで読んでから読者が一人ひとり埋めればよい隙間がある（正解はたぶんない）。
❻ invited me over: 僕を家に招いてくれた
❼ I'd never had a teacher invite me ...: have ＋人＋動詞 で「〜に...してもらう」。

今夜、小雨がたえまなく降りつづけ、街灯の光も霧に煙り、雨を集める光の漏斗のように見える。ここはファーウェル。アパートに並んだバルコニーの窓が、濡れたテニスコートに映っている。それはかつて僕の友バボヴィッチが住んでいたアパートだ。僕はふと思った。いつかは僕もこの町を去るのだろうか？　バボに会いに、はじめてファーウェルを歩いた晩のことを僕は思い出した。バボは僕が受講していたロシア文学のゼミの先生で、僕を家に招待してくれたのだ。先生に招かれるなんて、はじめての体験だった。「いつがいいですか？」と僕は訊ねた。

「お客はいつだって歓迎さ」と彼は答え、住所を紙になぐり書きした。「電話はないよ」

　冬の晩で、雪が降っていた。バボのアパートは通りのいちばん奥にあった。道はそこで湖につき当たって行きどまりになっていた。雪がびっしり貼りついた金網の向こう側で、テニスコートも、吹きよせた雪に包まれていた。コートと小さな湖畔の公園の先には白い桟橋があって、緑の灯台の光に

---

❽ "I can *always* use the company," he answered: 正しくは "I can always use company." これでバボにとって英語が母語でないことが示唆される。use は口語で can か could を伴い「〜があると嬉しい、〜は歓迎だ」、company は「お客」。

❾ scrawling out his address: 住所を走り書きして

❿ the last one on the block: 四つ角から四つ角までを a block といい、アメリカではきわめて日常的に使われる。

⓫ dead-end(ed): 行き止まる

⓬ a snow-clotted cyclone fence: 雪が固まって貼りついた金網。cyclone fence は元は商品名だが要するに「金網」。

⓭ drifted over: drifted over by snow ということ。drift は雪などを「吹き寄せる」で、over があるので吹き寄せられた雪が全体を包んでいる感じ。

⓮ (a) pier: 桟橋

⓯ (a) beacon: 灯台

9

^❶obliterated the outlines of sidewalks and ^❷curbs and that night the pier looked as if it was ^❸a continuation of the street, as if Farwell ^❹lengthened out into the lake. I walked out toward the beacon. Ice, ^❺sculpted by waves and ^❻spray, ^❼encrusted the pier.
5 The guard cables and beacon tower ^❽were sheathed in ice. In the frozen quiet, I could hear the lake ^❾rasping in under the ^❿floes and feel the pier ^⓫shudder, and as I walked back toward the apartment building I thought I heard singing.

The baritone voice ^⓬resonating across the tennis courts seemed
10 to float from a balcony window where a curtain ^⓭fluttered out as if signalling. I was sure it was Babo's window. Instead of ringing his bell, I stood on the tennis court and tried to ^⓮make out the song, but the words were ^⓯indistinct. I formed a snowball out of fresh snow—snow too ^⓰feathery to be ^⓱good packing—and ^⓲lobbed it
15 at the window. It exploded against ^⓳the pane with a soft ^⓴*phoom*.
I ^㉑expected Babo to come to the window. Instead, the music

---

❶ obliterated the outlines: 輪郭を抹消していた

❷ curb(s): 車道と歩道を仕切るために並べた四角い石のこと。

❸ a continuation: 続き

❹ lengthen(ed): 延びている

❺ sculpt(ed): 〜を彫る（sculpture〔＝彫刻〕から）

❻ spray: 水しぶき

❼ encrust(ed): 〜を殻で覆う

❽ were sheathed in ...: 〜で覆われていた。sheathe は刀を鞘に納めるイメージ。

❾ rasp(ing): きしる

❿ floe(s): 浮氷。"in under the floes" は浮氷の下にある湖の中、というイメージで、氷の下に水が閉じ込められている感じがよく伝わってくる。

⓫ shudder: 身震いする

向かって伸びていた。雪が舗道や縁石の輪郭を消し去っていて、その晩は桟橋も道路のつづきのように見えた。まるでファーウェルがそのまま湖までつき出しているみたいだった。僕は灯台の光の方に歩いていった。波としぶきに削られた氷が、甲羅のように桟橋を覆っていた。安全用ケーブルも灯台の塔も、氷のさやに包まれていた。何もかもが凍りついた静けさのなか、浮氷の下で湖がきしむのが聞こえた。桟橋がぶるっと震えるのが感じられた。僕はアパートの方に戻りはじめた。と、歌声が聞こえたような気がした。

　テニスコートの向こう側から響いてくるそのバリトンは、合図でも送るみたいにカーテンがひらひら揺れているバルコニーの窓から漂ってくるらしかった。きっとあれがバボの部屋だ。呼鈴を鳴らす代わりに、僕はテニスコートに立ち、それが何の歌か聞きとろうとしたが、歌詞はぼんやりとしか伝わってこなかった。僕は降りたての雪で雪玉をつくり——よく締まった玉をつくるにはふわふわすぎる雪だ——それを窓めがけて山なりに投げ上げた。玉は窓に命中し、柔らかなふうんという音を立てた。これでバボも窓辺に出てくるだろう、と僕は思った。ところが代わりに、音楽がやんだ。僕は雪玉

⓬ resonating <resonate: 鳴り響く

⓭ fluttered out: 外向けにひらひら揺れた

⓮ make out: 読みにくい字を「読みとる」、聞きにくい音を「聞きとる」といった意味で、非常によく使う。

⓯ indistinct: ぼんやりした（↔ distinct）

⓰ feathery: feather（羽根）のようにふわっとした

⓱ good packing: よく締まった（雪）玉

⓲ lob(bed): 〜をふわっと山なりに投げる

⓳ the pane: 窓ガラス

⓴ phoom: 雪玉が窓に当たった音を模している。

㉑ expected Babo to come ...: expected は「期待した」ではなく「予想した」。

stopped. I lobbed another snowball and the bronze light inside the apartment ❶flicked off. ❷Finally, I walked around to the entrance hall and ❸buzzed the bell beside the name Andrei Babovitch, but there was no answer. ❹I was about to give up when I saw his face
5 ❺magnified by the beveled panes of the lobby door. He opened the door and ❻broke into ❼the craggy grin I'd seen possess his face in class when he would ❽read a poem aloud—first in Russian, as if ❾chanting, and then translated into his ❿hesitant, British-accented English.

10 ⓫"So, you," he said.

"Is it a good night for a visit?"

"⓬Definitely. Come in, please. Have tea. And ⓭a little shot of something to warm up."

"I thought I guessed which window was yours and threw
15 snowballs to ⓮get your attention."

---

❶ flicked off: パチンと消えた
❷ Finally: しばし待ってみたあとに、という感じ。
❸ buzzed the bell beside the name Andrei Babovitch: アンドレイ・バボヴィッチと書いてある横のベルを鳴らした。the entrance hall（玄関ホール）に、各部屋の呼び鈴のボタンが並んでいて、それぞれの横に名前を書いた紙を差し込むようになっている。
❹ I was about to give up when ...: 「〜したとき僕はあきらめようとしていた」ではなく、「あきらめようとしたら〜した」。
❺ magnified by the beveled panes: 面取りしたガラスに拡大されて
❻ broke into the craggy grin: にっといかつい笑みを浮かべた。break into はそのあとに laughter, tears などが来て「わっと笑い出す／泣き出す」等々。
❼ the craggy grin I'd seen possess his face in class: 直訳すれば「授業中に彼の顔に取り憑くのを僕が見ていたいかつい笑み」。"the man I saw shoot the policeman"（警官を撃つところを私が見た男）などと同じ構造。

12

をもうひとつ投げ上げた。と、アパートのなかのブロンズ色の明かりがぱっと消えた。僕はしかたなくアパートの玄関に回っていって、アンドレイ・バボヴィッチと書かれたかたわらのベルを押した。返事はなかった。あきらめて帰ろうとしたところで、ロビーのドアにはめた面取りガラスに、バボの顔が拡大されて映っているのが見えた。ドアを開けた彼は、にやっといかつく笑ってみせた。それは僕にも見覚えのある笑顔だった。教室で詩を朗読するとき——まずはじめにロシア語で歌うように、それからためらいがちにイギリスなまりの英語に翻訳するのだ——バボの顔に現われる笑顔である。

「やあ、君か」と彼は言った。

「今晩でよかったでしょうか？」

「もちろんだとも。さあ、お入り。お茶を入れよう。それと、強いのを一杯引っかけて体を温めたまえ」

「どの窓が先生の部屋か見当をつけて、呼鈴代わりに雪玉を投げたんですけど」

❽ read a poem aloud:「大声で読む」ではなく「声に出して読む」。

❾ chant(ing): フランス語の chanter（歌う）から来ていて（さらにラテン語の cantāre にさかのぼる）、しばしば宗教的な響きがあり、「唱える」というニュアンスを伴った「歌う」。

❿ hesitant: ためらい気味の

⓫ "So, you," he said: ここでもバボの英語はおよそ流暢ではない。直前に British-accented English（イギリス訛りの英語）とあるが、完璧なイギリス英語が身に付いているわけではない。

⓬ Definitely: もちろん

⓭ a little shot of something:「何かのちょっとした一杯」。ビール、ワインなどは shot とは言わない。ウォッカのように、一口飲んだだけで温まりそうな酒について言う。

⓮ get your attention: あなたの気を引く

"That was you! I thought ❶hooligans ❷had heard Chaliapin moaning about fate and ❸become enraged. Russian opera can have that effect even on those not ❹addicted to rock and roll. I didn't know what to expect next—❺a brick, maybe—so I turned off the music and laid down on the floor in the dark."

"Sorry," I said, "I wasn't thinking—I don't know why I didn't just ring the bell."

"No, no. ❻It would have been a memorable entrance. I'm sorry I missed it, though if I looked out the window and saw you in the dark I still might have thought it was hooligans," he laughed. "As you see, ❼my nerves aren't what they should be."

The bronze light ❽was back on ❾in his apartment, which seemed ❿furnished in books. Books in various languages⓫lined the walls and ⓬were stacked along the floor. His ⓭furniture was ⓮crates of more books, ⓯the stock left from a small Russian bookstore he'd opened then closed after receiving ⓰ threats and a bomb in the

---

❶ hooligan(s): ヨーロッパではサッカー場で暴れる観客について言うことが多いが、元々はごろつき一般を指す語。

❷ had heard Chaliapin moaning about fate: シャリアピンが運命を嘆くのを聞いた。シャリアピンは1900〜30年代に活躍し絶大な人気を誇ったロシアのオペラ歌手。1936年に来日し、彼の歯痛に帝国ホテル料理長が配慮したことで「シャリアピン・ステーキ」が生まれた。

❸ become enraged: 激昂する

❹ addicted to rock and roll: ロックンロールに中毒している。ダイベックは1942年生まれでもあり、この物語全体、ビートルズらが登場しロックンロールが「ロック」になる以前の時代を感じさせる。

❺ a brick: 煉瓦

❻ It would have been a memorable entrance:「記憶すべき登場となったところだろう」。もし雪玉に応えて、窓から外に姿を見せていたらということ。

「何だ、君だったのか！ 私はまた、シャリアピンが運命を嘆くのを聞いた不良どもが怒り狂ったのかと思ったよ。ロシアオペラというのは、ロックンロールに中毒していない人間にもそういう効果を及ぼすことがあるものでね。つぎは何が来るかと思ったよ――煉瓦かな、とね。それで音楽を止めて部屋を暗くして、床に伏せたわけさ」

「すいません」と僕は言った。「何も考えてなかったんです――どうして素直に呼鈴を鳴らさなかったのかな」

「いやいや。うまくいけばこっちも、千両役者堂々たる登場、だったろうにな。チャンスを逸して残念だね。もっとも、窓から顔を出して、闇のなかに君がいるのが見えたとしても、やっぱり不良どもだと思ったかもしれんが」彼はそう言って笑った。「ごらんのとおり、私の神経はいささかくたびれていてね」

ブロンズの明かりがふたたび部屋にともっていた。バボの部屋は、書物が家具代わりに並んでいるという感じだった。さまざまな言語の本が壁を埋め、床にもびっしり積まれていた。家具と見えるのも、要するにさらなる本の箱だった。かつて彼が開いた小さなロシア語書店のストックの残りである。脅迫状が何通も送られてきて――一度は爆弾も送られてきた――店じまいせ

---

❼ my nerves aren't what they should be: 直訳すれば「私の神経はそれらが本来そうであるべきものではない」＝「神経がいささか損なわれている」。

❽ was back on: ふたたび灯っていた

❾ in his apartment: アパート全体を言うときは apartment building/house であり、apartment だけだとこのようにアパートの中の一世帯分を言う。

❿ furnished: 家具が付いている。普通はそのあとに in books とは続かない。

⓫ lined the walls: 壁に沿って並んでいた

⓬ were stacked: 積み上げられていた

⓭ furniture: 家具

⓮ crate(s): （運搬用の大きな）木箱

⓯ the stock: 在庫

⓰ threat(s): 脅迫

mail. Above his desk, he'd ❶tacked a street map of Odessa, where he'd grown up beside the Black Sea. There were circles of red ink along a few of the streets. I didn't ask that night, but later, when I knew him better, I asked what the red circles ❷marked.

5   ❸"Good bakeries," he said.

When the university ❹didn't renew his contract, he moved away suddenly. It didn't surprise me. He'd ❺been on the move since ❻deserting to the British during the War. He'd lived in England, and Canada, and said he never knew where else was 10 next, but that sooner or later staying in one place reminded him that ❼where he belonged no longer existed. He'd lived on Farwell, ❽a street whose name sounded almost like saying goodbye.

Tonight, I ❾jogged down Farwell to the lake, past the ❿puddled tennis courts and the pier with its green beacon, and then along 15 ⓫the empty beach. Waves were rushing in and I ran as if ⓬being chased, ⓭tightroping along ⓮the foaming edge of water. My shoes

---

❶ tack(ed): 〜を画鋲で留める

❷ mark(ed): 〜をしるす

❸ "Good bakeries," he said: たとえば "Good bookstores"（よい本屋）ではなく「よいパン屋」であることが、失われたものの大きさをより切実に感じさせる。

❹ didn't renew his contract: 契約を更新してくれなかった。正規の教授であれば tenure といって一生在職する権利を与えられることが多いが、バボは一年ごとに契約を更新する一介の講師だった。

❺ (had) been on the move: ずっと動きつづけていた

❻ desert(ing): 脱走する

❼ where he belonged no longer existed:「彼の属している場所はもはや存在しなかった」。where he belonged あたり、改まった言い方とは言いがたく、

ざるをえなかったのだ。机の上の壁には、オデッサの市街図が画鋲で止めて
あった。黒海に面したこの町が、バボの生まれ故郷だった。二、三の道路沿
いに、赤インクでいくつか丸が書きこんであった。その晩には訊かなかった
けれど、あとでもっと親しくなってから、赤丸は何のしるしなのか僕は訊ね
てみた。

「おいしいパン屋だよ」と彼は答えた。

　大学に契約を更新してもらえなかったとき、バボはあっさりよそへ移って
いった。僕は驚かなかった。戦争中に英国軍に脱走して以来、彼はずっと動
きつづけてきたのだ。イギリスに住んだこともあれば、カナダに住んだこと
もあった。つぎはどこなのか見当もつかんよ、と彼は言っていた。でもね、
ひとつの場所にとどまっていると、いずれ遅かれ早かれ、自分が属す場所
がもうなくなってしまったことを思い出してしまうんだよ、と。そして彼は
ファーウェルに住んだ。さようなら、と言っているような名前の通りに。

　今夜、僕はファーウェルを走って湖まで行った。水たまりのできたテニス
コートの前を通り、緑の灯台のある桟橋を過ぎ、人けのない岸辺を走った。
波が打ちよせていた。誰かに追われているみたいに、泡立つ波打ちぎわを綱

間接話法ではあれ、バボの素朴な言い方が反映されているように思える。

❽ a street whose name sounded almost like saying goodbye: 言うまで
もなく、Farwell という通りの名は farewell（さらば）を連想させる。なお
Farwell はシカゴ北部に実在する通りであり、テニスコート、桟橋、灯台など
もこの小説で描写されているとおり。

❾ jogged down Farwell: ファーウェルをジョギングした

❿ puddled: 水たまりになった

⓫ the empty beach: 言うまでもなくシカゴはミシガン湖に面しているので
beach は「湖岸」。

⓬ be(ing) chased: 追われる

⓭ tightroping along ...: 〜沿いを綱渡りし（綱渡りするように進み）

⓮ the foaming edge of water: 泡立つ波打ちぎわの水

❶peeled flying **❷**clods of footprints from the sand. It was late by the time I reached the building where I lived, **❸**the hallways quiet, supper smoke still **❹**ringing the lightbulbs. In the dark, my room with its windows raised smelled of wet **❺**screens and **❻**tangerines.

5

10

15

❶ peel(ed): 〜を剥がす、剥ぐ
❷ clods of footprints: 足あとのかたまり。clod は土のかたまりを言うことが多い。
❸ the hallway(s): 玄関、廊下
❹ ringing the lightbulbs: 電球を輪のように囲んで
❺ screen(s): 網戸
❻ tangerine(s): タンジェリン（日本のミカンに似ている）

渡りするように僕は走った。靴が砂から足跡の塊をひき剝がしていった。自分のアパートに戻ったのは、もう遅い時間だった。廊下は静かで、夕食のなごりの煙が電球を包んでいた。暗闇のなかで、窓を開け放った僕の部屋は、濡れた網戸とミカンの匂いがした。

ちなみに

　Dybek とはポーランド系の名前であり、ポーランド語では「ディベ
ク」だがアメリカでは誰もが「ダイベック」と読んでしまうのでそれ
に合わせている。ダイベックが子供のころよく一緒に過ごした祖母は
英語がひとことも喋れず、スチュアート少年はポーランド語がひとこ
とも喋れなかったが、二人は完璧に意思が交わせたという。言葉を超
えて伝わるものへのあこがれはダイベックの作品全体を貫いている。

You Are Not I
Paul Bowles

あんたはあたしじゃない

ポール・ボウルズ

★ ★ ☆

ポール・ボウルズ

(Paul Bowles, 1910-1999)

ニューヨーク出身の作家・作曲家。まず作曲家として地位を築いたのち、1947 年、タンジールに移住、以後、西洋文明が強烈な他者性を帯びた人や場に出会う物語を数多く著した。"You Are Not I" は1948 年、ボウルズが見た夢に基づいて書かれたという。これを含め主な短篇は Collected Stories, 1939–1976 (1979) に収められ、長篇に The Sheltering Sky (1949) など。

Y ou are not I. ❶No one but me could ❷possibly be. I know that,
and I know where I have been and what I have done ever
since yesterday when I ❸walked out the gate during ❹the train
wreck. Everyone was so excited that no one noticed me. I became
5 completely unimportant as soon as it was a question of ❺cut
people and smashed cars down there on the tracks. We girls all went
running down ❻the bank when we heard the noise, and we ❼landed
against ❽the cyclone fence like a lot of monkeys. Mrs. Werth ❾was
chewing on her crucifix and ❿crying her eyes out. ⓫I suppose it
10 hurt her lips. Or maybe she thought one of her daughters was on
the train down there. It was really a bad accident; anyone could
see that. The spring rains ⓬had dissolved the earth that kept the
ties firm, and so the rails had spread a little and the train had gone
into ⓭the ditch. But ⓮how everyone could get so excited I still fail
15 to understand.

I always hated the trains, hated to see them ⓯go by down there,

❶ No one but me could ...: 私以外誰も～できない
❷ possibly: 否定文にこの語が入ると否定が強まる。
❸ walked out the gate: 門から歩いて出た。"look out the window" "run out
the room" などと同じ用法。
❹ the train wreck: 列車事故
❺ cut people and smashed cars: 切り傷を負った人々と、壊れた車両（cars
は「自動車」ではない）
❻ the bank: 土手
❼ land(ed): 着地する
❽ the cyclone fence: 金網（p. 8, l. 14 と同じ）
❾ was chewing on her crucifix: 十字架（のペンダント）を噛んでいた
❿ crying her eyes out: 泣きじゃくって（文字どおりには「目玉が落ちてしまう
ほど泣いて」）

あんたはあたしじゃない。あたし以外だれもあたしになれっこない。あたしにはそのことがわかってる。それにあたしは、きのう、列車事故のすきに門を抜け出してから、じぶんがどこで、なにをしていたか、それもちゃんとわかってる。みんなすごく興奮していたから、だれもあたしに目もくれなかった。あの線路の上で、人がおおぜい怪我をして、車両がめちゃめちゃに壊れたせいで、あたしのことなんかまるっきりどうでもよくなってしまったのだ。衝突の音を聞いて、あたしたち女の子はいっせいに土手をかけ下りて、猿の群れみたいに金網にへばりついた。ミセス・ワースは十字架を噛みながら、目を真赤に泣きはらしていた。きっと唇が痛かったのだろう。それともあの列車にじぶんの娘が乗っているとでも思ったのかもしれない。それはほんとうにひどい事故だった。だれが見てもまちがいなくひどい事故だった。春の雨のせいで、枕木を支えている土が柔らかくなって、それでレールが広がって列車が溝に落ちてしまったのだ。でもどうしてみんなあんなに興奮できるのか、あたしにはいまだにわからない。

あたしは前から列車が嫌いだった。列車があそこを通りすぎるのを見る

❶❶ I suppose it hurt her lips. Or maybe she thought …: 悲惨な事故を目にして泣いている人を見て、おおかたペンダントを噛んで唇が痛いのか、それとも自分の娘が事故に遭ったと思ったのだろう、と語り手は言う。これが辛辣な皮肉なのか、それとも彼女のいささか異様な思考を伝えているのか、この時点では（あるいは最後まで）わからない。

❶❷ had dissolved the earth that kept the ties firm:（普段は）枕木（the ties）をしっかり押さえている土を緩ませてしまっていた

❶❸ the ditch: 溝

❶❹ how everyone could get so excited I still fail to understand: ここでも、悲惨な事故が起きた事態について、「何をそんなに騒ぐのかわからない」と語り手は言っている（ちなみに普通の語順なら "I still fail to understand how everyone could get so excited."）。

❶❺ go by: 通り過ぎていく

hated to see them disappear ❶ way off up the valley toward the next town. It made me angry to think of all those people moving from one town to another, ❷ without any right to. ❸ Whoever said to them: "You may go and buy your ticket and make the trip this
5 morning to ❹ Reading. You will ❺ go past twenty-three stations, over forty bridges, through three tunnels, and still keep going, if you want to, even after you get to Reading"? No one. I know that. I know there is no chief who says things like that to people. But it makes it ❻ pleasanter for me when I imagine such a person does
10 exist. Perhaps it would be only a ❼ tremendous voice speaking ❽ over a public-address system set up in all the main streets.

When I saw the train down there ❾ helpless ❿ on its side like ⓫ an old worm knocked off a plant, I began to laugh. But I ⓬ held on to the fence very hard when the people started to ⓭ climb out the
15 windows bleeding.

⓮ I was up in the courtyard, and there was the paper wrapper

---

❶ way off up the valley: 谷間のずっと上の方で。way は "way down in the valley"（はるか下の谷間）"way across the ocean"（はるか海の彼方）などと同じ用法。off はなくてもほとんど変わらないが、距離感がより強まる。

❷ without any right to: そうする（町から町へ移る）権利などないのに

❸ Whoever said to them ...?: いったいどこの誰に〜と言われたのか

❹ Reading: レディング（「リーディング」ではない）。ロンドンの西にある町がおそらく一番よく知られているが、マサチューセッツ、オハイオ、ペンシルヴェニアにもある。

❺ go past twenty-three stations, over forty bridges, through three tunnels: 作者にはむろんそんな意図はなかっただろうが、「〜を通って」というときに past, over, through がどう使い分けられるかに関する、お手本のような文になっている（横を通る／上を通る／中を通る）。

のも、隣り町に向かって谷間のずっと奥のほうに消えていくのを見るのも嫌だ。あそこに乗ってる、なんの権利もないくせに町から町へと動いていく連中のことを考えると、あたしは腹が立ってしかたがなかった。いったいだれに言われたっていうのか、「おまえはきょう切符を買ってレディングまで行ってよろしい。道中おまえは二十三の駅を通過して、四十の橋を渡り、三つのトンネルを通り抜けるであろう。それでもまだ行きたければ、レディングに着いてもなお先へ進んでよろしい」なんて、だれが言ってくれたっていうのか？ そんなことだれも言いやしない。あたしにはわかってる。そういうことをみんなに言ってくれる、親分みたいな人なんか、どこにもいやしない。でも、もしそんな人がほんとにいたら、なんて想像すると楽しい。もしかしたらそれは声だけの存在かもしれない。町じゅうの大通りに据えつけたスピーカーから流れる、とてつもなく大きな声。

　老いぼれの毛虫が枝からたたき落とされたみたいに、ぶざまに横たわっている列車を見て、あたしは笑ってしまった。でも、血を流した乗客たちが窓からはい出してくると、あたしはしっかり金網にへばりついた。

　あたしは中庭にいて、チーズクラッカーの包み紙がベンチの上に転がって

---

❻ pleasanter: pleasant の比較級は more pleasant と pleasanter の二つがありうるが、pleasanter を「間違っている」と感じる人も少なくないと思われる。

❼ tremendous: ものすごく大きな

❽ over a public-address system: PA システムで

❾ helpless: 無力で、なすすべもなく

❿ on its side: 横倒しになって

⓫ an old worm knocked off a plant: 植物から叩き落とされた、老いた毛虫

⓬ held on to ...: 〜にしがみついた

⓭ climb out the windows: このように climb は「登る」より「這う」と考えた方がピンと来る場合も多い。out は p. 22, l. 3 に同じ。

⓮ I was up in the courtyard ... Then I was at the main gate: 語り手はあれよあれよという間に場を移動していく。どこか現実感がないようにも思える。

off a box of ❶Cheese Tid Bits lying on the bench. Then I was at the main gate, and it was open. A black car was outside ❷at the curb, and a man was sitting in front smoking. I thought of speaking to him and asking him if he knew who I was, but I decided not
5 to. It was a sunny morning full of sweet air and birds, I followed the road around the hill, down to the tracks. Then I ❸walked up the tracks feeling excited. The dining car looked strange lying on its side with the window glass all broken and ❹some of the cloth shades drawn down. ❺A robin kept whistling in a tree above.
10 "Of course," I said to myself. "This is just in man's world. ❻If something real should happen, they would stop singing." I walked up and down along ❼the cinder bed beside the track, looking at the people lying in the bushes. Men were beginning to carry them up toward ❽the front end of the train where the road crosses the
15 tracks. There was a woman in a white uniform, and I tried to ❾keep from passing close to her.

---

❶ Cheese Tid Bit(s): ナビスコ社が販売していたスティック状のスナック。

❷ at the curb: 道端に。curb は p. 10, l. 1 に同じ。

❸ walked up the tracks: 線路を歩いていった。線路が上り坂になっているとは限らない。

❹ some of the cloth shades drawn down: 布製のブラインドがいくつか引き下げられて

❺ A robin: コマドリ

❻ If something real should happen: もし何か本当のことが起きたら。つまり（鳥の身になっている）彼女の感覚では、列車事故は real ではなく "just in man's world" の出来事でしかない。

❼ the cinder bed: 石炭の燃え殻（cinder）を敷いた線路の道床。

❽ the front end: 先頭

いた。それからあたしは正門にいて、門はあいていた。表の道ばたに、黒い車がとまっていて、運転席に男が一人すわって煙草を喫っていた。あたしはその男に声をかけてあたしがだれだかわかるか訊いてみようかと思ったけど、やっぱりやめにした。晴れた朝で、空気はいい匂いだし鳥もたくさん飛びかっていた。あたしは道にそって丘をぐるっとまわり、線路まで降りていった。あたしはわくわくしながら線路の上を歩いていった。食堂車が横倒しになっているのって、なんだかすごく奇妙なながめだった。窓ガラスはぜんぶ割れていて、布のシェードはいくつか下りていた。木の上でコマドリが一羽さえずっていた。「そりゃそうよね」とあたしは思った。「こんなの人間の世界だけの出来事なんだ。もしほんとになにかが起きたら、鳥だって歌うのをやめるはずだ」。あたしは線路のわきの、石炭殻の土台の上を行ったり来たりしながら、草むらに倒れている人たちをながめた。男たちがその人たちを車両の前方の、踏切があるほうに運びはじめた。白い制服を着た女が一人いた。あたしはなるべくその女に近よらないようにした。

❾ keep from passing close to her: 彼女の近くを通ることを避ける

I decided to go down a wide ❶path that led through the blackberry bushes, and in a small ❷clearing I found an old ❸stove with a lot of dirty bandages and handkerchiefs in the ❹rubbish around the base of it. ❺Underneath everything was a pile of stones.

5 I found several round ones and some others. The earth here was very soft and moist. When I got back to the train there seemed to be a lot more people running around. I walked close to the ones who were ❻lying side by side on the cinders, and looked at their faces. One was a girl and her mouth was open. I❼dropped one of

10 the stones in and went on. A fat man also had his mouth open. I put in a sharp stone that looked like a piece of coal. ❽It occurred to me that I might not have enough stones for them all, and the cinders were too small. There was one old woman ❾walking up and down wiping her hands on her skirt very quickly, over and

15 over again. She ❿had on a long black silk dress with ⓫a design of blue mouths stamped all over it. Perhaps they ⓬were supposed to

---

❶ (a) path: 野山の道、小道
❷ (a) clearing: 森の中の、木を少し伐採した空き地
❸ (a) stove: 調理用のレンジ。薪ストーブなら英語でも stove だが、電気ストーブなどは heater。
❹ rubbish: ゴミ
❺ Underneath everything was a pile of stones: その全部の下に小石の山があった。a pile of stones が主語。
❻ lying side by side: 並んで横たわって
❼ dropped one of the stones in: 石をひとつ中に落とした
❽ It occurred to me ...: 「全員分の石はないかもしれない」と思う「あたし」にとっては、怪我人や死者の口に石を入れていくことが何より自然なことのようである。その意図や象徴的意味を考えたくなるが、そのように外からこの人を眺め

あたしはブラックベリーの茂みを抜ける広い山道を行くことにした。途中
小さく拓けた場所があって、そこに古い調理台が捨ててあった。調理台の下
はゴミが山になっていて、汚い包帯やハンカチがいっぱいあった。一番下に
は小石が積みかさなっていた。あたしはまん丸の石をいくつか、それ以外の
をいくつか選んだ。このあたりの土はとても柔らかくて、じっとり湿ってい
た。汽車のところに戻ると、走りまわっている人の数がさっきよりずっと増
えたみたいだった。あたしは石炭殻の上に並んで横たわっている人たちのそ
ばへ寄っていって、その人たちの顔をのぞいてみた。一人は女の子で、口が
ぱっくりあいていた。あたしは石を一つ、その口のなかに落として、先へ進
んだ。太った男がやっぱり同じように口をあけていた。あたしは石炭のかけ
らみたいに鋭くとがった石をそこへ入れた。この調子じゃ石が足りないかも
しれない、とあたしはふと思った。かといって石炭殻じゃ小さすぎるし。年
とった女が一人、そのへんを行ったり来たりしながらスカートで両手を何
度もせわしなく拭いていた。女は長い黒の絹のワンピースを着ていて、ワン
ピースには一面、青い口の模様が入っていた。もしかしたら葉っぱのつもり

るより、まずはこの人に「なってみる」のがこの時点では得策ではないかと思う。

❾ walking up and down: 行ったり来たりして

❿ had on ...: 〜を着ていた

⓫ a design of blue mouths stamped all over it: 青い口の模様が一面にプリン
トされて

⓬ were supposed to be ...: 〜のつもりだった

be leaves but they were formed like mouths. She looked crazy to me and I kept clear of her. Suddenly I noticed a hand with rings on the fingers ❶sticking out from under a lot of ❷bent pieces of metal. I ❸tugged at the metal and saw a face. It was a woman and her
5 mouth was closed. I tried to open it ❹so I could get a stone in. A man ❺grabbed me by the shoulder and ❻pulled at me. He looked angry. "What are you doing?" he yelled. "Are you crazy?" I began to cry and said she was my sister. She did look a little like her, and I sobbed and kept saying: "She's dead. She's dead." The man
10 stopped looking so angry and ❼pushed me along toward the head of the train, holding my arm tightly with one hand. I tried to ❽jerk away from him. At the same time I decided not to say anything more except "She's dead" ❾once in a while. "That's all right," the man said. When we got to the front end of the train he made me sit
15 down on ❿the grass embankment ⓫alongside a lot of other people. Some of them were crying, so I stopped and watched them.

---

❶ sticking out from under ...: 〜の下から突き出ていて
❷ bent: ひん曲がった（bend の過去分詞）
❸ tugged at ...: 〜をぐいぐい引っぱった
❹ so I could get a stone in: 石を中に入れられるように。改まった書き方なら so that I could ... だが、現代では that なしで言うことが多い。
❺ grab(bed): （乱暴に）〜を摑む
❻ pulled at me: 私の体を引っぱった、私を引き寄せようとした
❼ pushed me along: 私を押していった
❽ jerk away: ぐいっと体を動かして離れる
❾ once in a while: ときどき
❿ the grass embankment: 草の生えた線路脇の土手
⓫ alongside: 〜と並んで

かもしれないけど、形はまるっきり口だった。女は頭がおかしいみたいだったので、あたしはなるべく近よらないようにした。突然、ぐちゃぐちゃに折れまがった金属の山の下から、いくつも指輪をつけた手が一本にょきっと出ているのにあたしは気がついた。金属を引っぱってみると、人の顔が見えた。女だった。口は閉じていた。あたしは石が入るようにとその口をあけようとした。一人の男があたしの肩を乱暴につかんで、体ごとぐいと引っぱった。男は怒っているみたいだった。「なんの真似だ？」と男はわめいた。「気でも狂ったのか？」。あたしは泣き出して、この人はあたしの姉さんなんですと言った。たしかにその女はあたしの姉に似ていなくもなかった。あたしはしくしく泣きながら、何度も「死んじゃったわ。死んじゃったわ」と言った。男は怖い顔をやめて、片手であたしの腕をしっかりつかみ、うしろから押すようにしてあたしを列車の一番前のところに連れていった。あたしは男の手をふりほどこうとした。と同時にあたしは、「死んじゃったわ」と時おりくり返す以外はなにも言わないことにした。「大丈夫だよ」と男は言った。列車の先頭にたどり着くと、人がたくさん土手の草の上にすわっていた。男はあたしをその人たちと並べてすわらせた。泣いてる人も何人かいた。それであたしは泣くのをやめて、その人たちをながめた。

It seemed to me that life outside was like life inside. There was always somebody to stop people from doing what they wanted to do. I smiled when I thought that this was **❶**just the opposite of what I had felt when I was still inside. Perhaps what we want to
5 do is wrong, but why should they always be the ones to decide? I began to consider this as I sat there pulling the little new **❷**blades of grass out of the ground. And I thought that **❸**for once *I* would decide what was right, and do it.

❹ It was not very long before several ambulances **❺**drove up.
10 They were for us, the row of people sitting on the bank, as well as for the ones lying around on **❻**stretchers and overcoats. I don't know why, since the people weren't in pain. Or perhaps they were. When a great many people are in pain together they aren't so likely to make a noise about it, probably because no one listens.
15 Of course I was in no pain at all. **❼**I could have told anyone that if I had been asked. But no one asked me. What they did ask me

---

❶ just the opposite: 正反対
❷ blade(s): (細長い) 草の葉
❸ for once: 今度ばかりは、今度こそ
❹ It was not very long before ...: 〜するまでにさほど長くはかからなかった、まもなく〜した
❺ drove up: (車が) 来て停まった
❻ stretcher(s): 担架
❼ I could have told anyone that if I had been asked: もし誰かに訊かれていたら、そう答えることができただろう

　どうやら外の暮らしも、なかの暮らしと変わらないみたいだった。やりたいようにやろうとすると、いつもだれかが邪魔するのだ。なかにいたころ思ってたのとはまるっきり反対だ、とあたしは思った。そう思いながら口元がゆるんだ。まああたしたちのやりたいことっていうのは悪いことなのかもしれない。だけどどうしていつもいつも、あいつらばかりいい悪いを決める？　土手に腰を下ろして、生え立ての草をむしり取りながら、あたしはそういうことを考えた。そしてあたしは思った。なにがいいのか、こんどばかりはこのあたしが決めるのだ、そしてそれを実行するのだ、と。

　まもなく、救急車が何台かやって来た。あたしたちみたいに土手にすわっている連中や、担架や外套の上に横になっている連中を連れに来たのだ。なぜだかはわからない。だってだれも痛がったりしていなかったから。あるいはほんとは痛かったのかもしれない。たくさんの人がいっしょになって痛がっていると、あんまり騒ぎたてたりはしないものだ。たぶんだれも聞いてくれないからだろう。もちろんあたしだってぜんぜん痛くなんかなかった。だれかにきかれたらきっとそう答えただろう。でもだれもそんなことはきかなかった。奴らがきいたのはあたしの住所だ。あたしは姉の住所を教え

was my address, and I gave my sister's address because it is only a half hour's drive. Besides, **❶**I stayed with her for quite a while before I **❷**went away, **❸**but that was years ago, I think. We all drove off together, some lying down inside the ambulances, and the
5 rest of us sitting on an uncomfortable bench **❹** in one that had no bed. The woman next to me must have been a foreigner; she was **❺** moaning like a baby, and there was not a drop of blood on her that I could see, anywhere. I **❻**looked her all over very carefully on the way, but she seemed to resent it, and **❼**turned her face the other
10 way, still crying. When we got to the hospital **❽**we were all taken in and examined. About me they just said: "**❾**Shock," and asked me again where I lived. I gave them the same address as before, and soon they took me out again and put me into the front seat of a sort of station wagon, between the driver and another man, **❿**an
15 attendant, I suppose. They both spoke to me about the weather, but I **⓫**knew enough not to **⓬**let myself be trapped **⓭**that easily. I

---

❶ I stayed with her: 彼女の家で暮らしていた

❷ went away: 施設に入ったことをやや遠回しに言っている。

❸ but that was years ago, I think: でもそれは何年も前のことだと思う。"I think" の一言から、彼女の意識・記憶にやや怪しい部分があることが示唆される。

❹ in one: in an ambulance

❺ moan(ing): うめく（ように泣く）

❻ looked her all over: 彼女の体をじろじろ眺め回した。"look him in the eye" などと同様に、look のあとに at がない表現。

❼ turned her face the other way: 顔をそむけた

❽ we were all taken in and examined: 私たちはみな収容され検査された

❾ Shock: 医学的な文脈では、日常的に使う「ショック」より意味が強く、何かが（それこそショックなどが）あって血圧が急激に低下し、さまざまな障害が起きる

た。そこなら車で三十分で行けるからだ。それにあたしは、なかに入るまえ、けっこう長いこと姉の家で暮らしていたのだ。まあもう何年も昔のことだと思うけど。あたしたちはみんないっしょに救急車に乗って出発した。何人かは救急車のなかで横になり、あとはみんな、ベッドのついていない一台に乗りこんで、すわり心地の悪いベンチに腰かけた。あたしの隣りにすわった女は外国人らしかった。女は赤ん坊みたいにううううと泣いていた。見たところどこからも血は出ていなかった。車が走りつづけるなか、あたしは女を隅から隅までじっくりながめた。女はそれが気にさわったらしく顔をそむけたが、あいかわらず泣くのはやめなかった。病院に着くとあたしたちはみんな収容されて、検査を受けた。あたしの番がくると連中は「ショックを受けたらしい」と言っただけで、家はどこかね、ともう一度きいた。あたしはさっきと同じ住所を教えた。じきそいつらはまたあたしを連れ出して、ステーションワゴンみたいな車の前部席の、運転手ともう一人の男——たぶん看護人だろう——のあいだにすわらせた。二人ともあたしに天気の話をしてきたけれど、あたしはそんなにかんたんにひっかかるような間抜けじゃない。ご

こと。

❿ an attendant: 看護人
⓫ knew enough not to ...: 〜しないくらいの知恵はあった。know enough というフレーズにおいて know は「知識」ではなく「知恵」の問題を言っている。
⓬ let myself be trapped: 自分が罠にかかるのを許す＝罠にはまる
⓭ that easily: そんなに簡単に。that は形容詞や副詞に付いて「それほど〜」の意。*Is he that stupid?*（あいつ、そこまで馬鹿なのか？）

know how the simplest subject can suddenly ❶twist around and choke you when you think you're quite safe. "She's dead," I said once, when we were halfway between the two towns. "Maybe not, maybe not," said the driver, as if he were talking to a child. I kept
5 my head down most of the time, but I managed to count the gas stations as we went along.

When we arrived at my sister's house the driver got out and rang the bell. I had forgotten that the street was so ugly. The houses were built ❷one against the other, all alike, ❸with only
10 a narrow cement walk between. And ❹each one was a few feet lower than the other, so that the long row of them looked like an enormous flight of stairs. The children were evidently allowed to ❺run wild over all ❻the front yards, and ❼there was no grass anywhere in sight, only mud.
15 My sister came to the door. The driver and she spoke a few words, and then I saw her look very worried very suddenly. She

---

❶ twist around and choke ...: 〜に巻きついて窒息させる
❷ one against the other: たがいにくっつき合って
❸ with only a narrow cement walk between: あいだに狭いセメントの通路があるだけで。walk は家のまわりの通路の意。
❹ each one was a few feet lower than the other, so that the long row of them looked like an enormous flight of stairs: それぞれの家が隣より何フィートか低くなっていて、それが長く連なって一続きの階段のように見えた。坂道なのでこう見えるのだろうが、あたかも本当にだんだん低くなっているような、やや現実感を揺さぶられる言い方。
❺ run wild: 好き勝手に遊び回る
❻ the front yard(s): 家の正面にある庭。普通は芝生や花壇がある。
❼ there was no grass anywhere in sight: どこにも芝生は見えなかった

くさいな話題でも、油断していると、あっというまに妙な具合になって、首を締めつけられてしまうのだ。二つの町のまんなかあたりまで来たころ、あたしは一度だけ「死んじゃった」と言った。「いやいやわからんよ、わからんもんだよ」と、子供にでも話しかけてるみたいな口調で運転手が言った。あたしはほとんどずっと下を向いてたけど、通りすぎるガソリンスタンドの数だけはちゃんとかぞえていた。

　姉の家に着くと、運転手は車を降りて呼鈴を鳴らした。このあたりがこんなに醜かったことをあたしは忘れていた。似たりよったりの家々がぴったりくっついて建っていて、すきまにセメント敷の細い通路があるだけだ。どの家もとなりの家より何フィートか低くなっていて、長くのびた家並全体が巨大な一つづきの階段みたいに見えた。子供たちがどの家の前庭も好き放題駆け回っているのか、芝生はどこにも見あたらず、地面はどこも泥ばかりだった。

　姉が玄関に出てきた。運転手と二言三言ことばをかわすと、姉の顔がさっと、すごく心配そうな表情になるのが見えた。姉は車のところにやって来て、

came out to the car and **❶**leaned in. She had new glasses, thicker than the others. She did not seem to be looking at me. Instead she said to the driver: "Are you *sure* she's all right?"

"**❷**Absolutely," he answered. "I wouldn't be telling you if she
5 wasn't. **❸**She's just been examined all over **❹**up at the hospital. It's just shock. **❺**A good rest will fix her up fine." The attendant got out, to **❻**help me out and up the steps, although I could have gone perfectly well **❼**by myself. I saw my sister looking at me **❽**out of the corner of her eye **❾**the same as she used to. When I was on the
10 porch I heard her whisper to the attendant: "**❿**She don't look well yet to *me*." He patted her arm and said: "She'll be fine. Just don't let her get excited."

"That's what they always said," she complained, "but **⓫**she just *does*."

15   The attendant got into the car. "She **⓬**ain't hurt at *all*, **⓭**lady."

---

❶ leaned in:（車の中に入るかのように）身を乗り出した

❷ Absolutely: もちろん。この男は主人公が脱走したことを知らないので、体に怪我はないと請け合っているが、姉は精神の方を心配している。

❸ She's just been examined all over: 体の隅々まで検査を受けたばかりだ

❹ up at the hospital: 病院で。up にそれほど強い意味はないが、ここより中心に近い場所という含み。

❺ A good rest will fix her up fine: たっぷりの休息が彼女をきちんと直すでしょう＝ゆっくり休めばよくなりますよ

❻ help me out and up the steps: 私が車から出て階段を上るのを（手を添えて）手伝う。steps はここでは道路から玄関へ上がる数段のこと。

❼ by myself: 自分一人で

❽ out of the corner of her eye: 目の端で、横目で

なかをのぞきこんだ。眼鏡が新しく変わっていた。まえのやつより厚い。姉はあたしのことなんかぜんぜん見てないみたいだった。そして運転手のほうを向いて言った。「本当に大丈夫なんですか、この子？」

「もちろんですとも」と運転手は答えた。「自信がなけりゃこんなこと言いやしません。病院で徹底的に検査したばかりなんですから。ショックを受けただけです。平気平気、ゆっくり休めばまたよくなりますよ」。看護人が車を降りて、あたしを車から降ろし、玄関の階段をのぼらせてくれた。やろうと思えばそんなこと一人で完璧にできるのだけど。姉が目のはしからあたしを見ているのがわかった。前にもよくこうやってあたしを見たものだ。ポーチにたどり着くと、姉が看護人にひそひそ声で言うのが聞こえた。「私には大丈夫とは見えませんけど」。看護人は姉の腕をぽんぽんとたたいて、「すぐよくなりますって。とにかく興奮させないように、それだけ気をつけてあげて下さい」と言った。

「いつも皆さんそうおっしゃるんですけどね」と姉はぐちっぽく言った。「でもけっきょくいつだって興奮しちまうんです、この子」

　看護人は車に乗りこんだ。「ねえ奥さん、この子はどこも怪我しちゃいな

---

❾ the same as she used to: 前にしていたのと同じように

❿ She don't look well yet to *me*: 私にはまだよくなったようには見えない。She doesn't でなく don't になっているのは教育程度を示唆する。また彼女の言葉にイタリクスが付されるのはこのページで3度あり、落着かない気分が伝わってくる。

⓫ she just *does*: とにかくそうなる（興奮する）のだ

⓬ ain't hurt at *all*: どこにも怪我はない。こちらも isn't hurt と言っていないことで教育程度が示唆される。

⓭ lady: 大人の女性に対する、ややぞんざいな呼びかけ。

He **❶**slammed the door.

❷"Hurt!" exclaimed my sister, watching the car. It drove off and she stood following it with her eyes until it got to the top of the hill and turned. I was still looking down at the porch floor
5 because I wasn't sure yet what was going to happen. I often feel that something is about to happen, and when I do, I stay perfectly still and **❸**let it go ahead. **❹**There's no use wondering about it or trying to stop it. At this time I had no particular feeling that a special event **❺**was about to come out, but I did feel that I would
10 be more likely to do the right thing if I waited and let my sister act first. She **❻**stood where she was, in her apron, **❼**breaking off **❽**the tips of the pussywillow stems that stuck out of the bush beside her. She still refused to look at me. Finally she **❾**grunted: "**❿**Might as well go on inside. It's cold out here." I opened the door and
15 walked in.

⓫Right away I saw she **⓬**had had the whole thing rebuilt, **⓭**only

---

❶ slam(med): 〜を乱暴に閉める
❷ "Hurt!" exclaimed my sister: 「怪我だって！」と姉は叫んだ。男が「体に怪我はない」の一点張りで帰ってしまったので、怪我なんかの話じゃないのに！と怒っている。
❸ let it go ahead: それが先へ進むままにさせる
❹ There's no use wondering: （どうなるのかと）いろいろ考えても仕方ない
❺ was about to come out: 今にも起ころうとしていた
❻ stood where she was: （さっきから）同じところに立っていた
❼ break(ing) off ...: 〜をちぎる、むしる
❽ the tips of the pussywillow stems: ネコヤナギの枝の先っぽ
❾ grunt(ed): つっけんどんに言う
❿ Might as well ...: 〜した方がいい。ほかにもっとましな選択肢がないので仕方

いんですよ」。そう言って彼はドアをばたんと閉めた。

「怪我がなによ！」と姉はさけんで、車をにらみつけた。車が走りさって、丘のてっぺんまで上りつめ、それからカーブを曲がるまで、姉はその動きを目で追っていた。あたしはまだうつむいてポーチの床を見ていた。これからどうなるのか、まだ見当がつかなかったからだ。あたしはよく、なにかがいまにも起こりそうだという予感を感じる。そんなときあたしは、ひたすらじっとして、それが起きるのを待つ。あれこれ悩んだり、それを止めようとしたってしょうがないのだ。でもこのときはべつに、なにか特別なことが起こりそうだという予感もなかった。でもこういう感じはあった。ここはひとつじっくり待って、姉に先にことを起こさせるにかぎる、そうすればきっとあたしの思いどおりにやれるはずだ、と。姉はエプロン姿でそこにつっ立ったまま、かたわらの茂みからつき出ているネコヤナギの芽をつまんでは、その先っぽをむしり取っていた。姉はあいかわらずあたしを見ようとしなかった。そしてとうとううなるように言った。「まあとにかくなかへ入ろうじゃないの。こんな寒いところにいてもしょうがないから」。あたしはドアをあけて家のなかに入った。

　なかに入ったとたん、姉が全体を建て替えたことがわかった。といっても

なくそうする、という含み。
⓫ Right away: すぐに、即座に
⓬ had had the whole thing rebuilt: 全体を改築させていた。have ＋物＋過去分詞で「〜を…させる」。
⓭ only backward: ただし反対に、鏡に映したみたいに。ここが一種鏡の世界であることが示される。

backward. There was always ❶a hall and a living room, except that the hall used to be on the left-hand side of the living room and now it was on the right. That made me wonder why I had failed to notice that the front door was now at the right end of the porch.

5 She had even ❷switched the stairs and fireplace around into each other's places. The furniture was the same, but each piece had been put into the position exactly opposite to the way it had been before. I decided to say nothing and let her ❸do the explaining ❹if she felt like it. It occurred to me that it must have cost her every

10 cent she had in the bank, and still it looked exactly the same as it had when she began. I kept my mouth shut, but I ❺could not help looking around with a good deal of curiosity to see ❻if she had carried out the reversal in every detail.

I went into the living room. The three big chairs around the

15 center table were still wrapped in old sheets, and the floor lamp by the ❼pianola had the same torn cellophane cover on its ❽shade. I

---

❶ a hall: 玄関から入ってすぐの廊下・通路のこと。
❷ switched the stairs and fireplace around: 階段と暖炉の位置を入れ替えた
❸ do the explaining: 説明を行なう
❹ if she felt like it: そうしたいなら
❺ could not help looking around: まわりを見回さずにいられなかった
❻ if she had carried out the reversal in every detail: 彼女がこの反転をすべ
ての細部において実行したのかどうか
❼ (a) pianola: 自動ピアノ。19世紀末から20世紀初頭にかけては一般家庭にも
広まっていたが、蓄音機やラジオが出てきて廃れた。
❽ (a) shade: (ランプの) シェード、かさ

前のをひっくり返しただけだ。廊下と居間、という組合せは同じだけど、前は廊下が居間の左側にあったのが、いまは右になっている。ということは玄関のドアも右はじに移ったわけで、どうしてさっきそのことに気づかなかったのかあたしはちょっと不思議だった。階段と暖炉までちゃんと位置を入れかえてある。家具自体は同じだが、置き場所はそれぞれ前とは正反対のところになっていた。あたしはなにも言わないことにした。説明したければ姉のほうから説明してくるだろう。きっと貯金もぜんぶ使っちゃったんだろうな、とあたしはふと思った。だけどこれじゃなにも変わってやしない。あたしは口を閉ざしていた。でもついつい、興味しんしんあたりをじろじろ見てしまうのだった。こまかい点一つひとつまで、すべて左右を逆転させてあるのだろうか？

　あたしは居間に入っていった。センターテーブルのまわりの三つの大きな椅子はまだ古シーツにくるんだままだったし、ピアノーラの脇のフロアランプのシェードには、まえと同じ破けたセロハンがかぶせてあった。あたしは

began to laugh, everything looked so comical backward. I saw her grab **❶**the fringe of the portiere and **❷**look at me hard. I went on laughing.

The radio next door was playing **❸**an organ selection. Suddenly
5 my sister said: "Sit down, Ethel. I've got something to do. **❹**I'll be right back." She went into the kitchen through the hall and I heard the back door open.

I knew already where she was going. She was afraid of me, and she wanted Mrs. Jelinek to come over. Sure enough, in a minute
10 they both came in, and my sister **❺**walked right into the living room this time. She looked angry now, but she had nothing to say. Mrs. Jelinek is **❻**sloppy and fat. She shook hands with me and said: "Well, well, **❼**old-timer!" I decided not to talk to her either because I distrust her, so I turned around and lifted the lid of the pianola.
15 I tried to push down some keys, but **❽**the catch was on and they were all stiff and wouldn't move. I closed the lid and **❾**went over

---

❶ the fringe of the portiere: 戸口に（のれんのように）掛けたカーテンの、裾の房飾り

❷ look at me hard: 私をじっと睨む

❸ an organ selection: オルガン曲集

❹ I'll be right back: すぐ戻る

❺ walked right into the living room this time: 今回は迷わず居間に入ってきた

❻ sloppy: だらしない、むさくるしい

❼ (an) old-timer: 古顔、なじみの人

❽ the catch was on: 停止装置が掛かっていた

❾ went over to see out the window: 窓の外を見に行った。over は窓辺まである程度距離があることを示唆する。

笑いだした。場所をひっくり返しただけで、なにもかもがすごく滑稽に見え
たのだ。姉が仕切りカーテンの房飾りをぎゅっとつかんで、あたしをにらみ
つけるのが見えた。あたしは笑うのをやめなかった。

　となりの家のラジオがオルガンの曲を流していた。だしぬけに姉が言った。
「すわんなさい、エセル。あたしちょっと用があるから。すぐ戻ってくる」。
姉は廊下を抜けて台所へ入っていった。裏手のドアがあく音が聞こえた。

　姉がどこへ行くつもりなのか、あたしにはよくわかっていた。姉はあたし
のことを怖がっている。それでミセス・ジェリネクに応援をたのみに行った
のだ。まもなく、思ったとおり二人そろってやって来た。こんどは姉もため
らわずまっすぐ居間へ入ってきた。顔は怒っているみたいだったけど、でも
なにも言わなかった。ミセス・ジェリネクというのはおとなりのグズでデブ
のおばさんだ。彼女はあたしと握手をして、「さてさて、古顔の御帰還ね！」
と言った。あたしは彼女とも口をきかないことにした。この女は信用できな
いからだ。それであたしは横をむいてピアノーラの蓋を持ちあげた。そして
鍵盤をいくつか押してみたが、ストッパーが掛かっていてどの鍵盤も動かな
かった。あたしは蓋を閉め、窓ぎわに行って外を見た。小さな女の子が一人、

to see out the window. A little girl ❶was wheeling a doll carriage along the sidewalk down the hill; she kept looking back at the tracks the wheels made when they left a wet part of the pavement and went onto ❷a dry patch. I was determined not to let Mrs.
5 Jelinek ❸gain any advantage over me, so I kept quiet. I sat down in ❹the rocker by the window and began to ❺hum.

Before long they started to talk to each other in low voices, but of course I heard everything they said. Mrs. Jelinek said: "I thought ❻they was keeping her." My sister said: "I don't know. So did I.
10 But the man kept telling me she was all right. ❼Huh! She's just the same." "❽Why, sure," said Mrs. Jelinek. They were quiet a minute.

"Well, I'm not going to ❾put up with it!" said my sister, suddenly. "❿I'm going to tell Dr. Dunn what I think of him."

"Call the Home," urged Mrs. Jelinek.

15 "I certainly am," my sister answered. "You stay here. ⓫I'll see if Kate's in." She meant Mrs. Schultz, who ⓬lives on the other side

---

❶ was wheeling a doll carriage: お人形の乳母車を押していた

❷ a dry patch: 濡れていない部分

❸ gain any advantage over me: 私より少しでも優位に立つ

❹ the rocker: 揺り椅子、ロッキングチェア

❺ hum: 鼻歌を歌う、ハミングする

❻ they was keeping her: この was も "She don't" や "She ain't" と同様の響き。

❼ Huh!: ケッ、フン！

❽ Why, sure: そうよ、もちろんよ。Why は驚き・承認・抗議・戸惑い等々、実にいろんな感情を伝えうる言葉。ここでは承認・同意。

❾ put up with ...: 〜に耐える

❿ I'm going to tell Dr. Dunn what I think of him: ドクター・ダンに私が彼をどう思っているか言ってやる＝彼に不満をぶちまけてやる

人形の乳母車を押しながら坂になった舗道を下っていった。女の子は何度も
うしろをふり返って、乳母車の車輪がのこした跡をながめた。乳母車が舗道
の濡れた部分から乾いた部分へ移動すると、そういう跡ができるのだ。あた
しはミセス・ジェリネクなんかにつけ込まれるまいと、一言もしゃべらず黙
りこくっていた。そして窓ぎわのロッキングチェアにすわり、小声でハミン
グしはじめた。

　まもなく二人はひそひそ声で内緒話をやり出した。でももちろん話の中味
はぜんぶあたしにも聞こえた。ミセス・ジェリネクは言った。「まだ入院し
てると思ってたのに」。姉は言った。「わけがわかんないわ。あたしだってそ
う思ってたわよ。だけど連れてきた男ったら大丈夫ですの一点ばりなの。よ
く言うわよ。ぜんぜん変わってないじゃないの」。「そうよ、そうよねえ」と
ミセス・ジェリネクが言った。二人はしばらく黙っていた。
「冗談じゃないわ、こんなの我慢できないわよ！」と姉がとつぜん言った。
「ドクター・ダンに文句言ってやらなきゃ」
「ホームに電話なさいよ」とミセス・ジェリネクも言った。
「もちろんよ」と姉は答えた。「あんたはここにいて。あたし、ケイトがい
るかどうか見てくる」。ケイトというのは反対隣のミセス・シュルツのこと

❶ I'll see if Kate's in: I'll see if Kate is in. （ケイトが家にいるか見てくる）
❷ lives on the other side: 反対側に住んでいる。ミセス・ジェリネクとは反対
　の隣ということ。

and has a telephone. I did not even look up when she went out. I
had made a big decision, and that was to **❶**stay right in the house
and **❷**under no condition let myself be taken back there. I knew it
would be difficult, but I had **❸**a plan I knew would work if I used
5 all my **❹**will power. I have great will power.

The first important thing to do was to **❺**go on keeping quiet,
not to speak a word that might **❻**break the spell I was starting to
work. I knew I would have to **❼**concentrate deeply, but that is easy
for me. I knew it was going to be a battle between my sister and
10 me, but **❽**I was confident that my **❾**force of character and superior
education **❿**had fitted me for just such a battle, and that I could
win it. All I had to do was to keep insisting inside myself, and
things would happen **⓫**the way I willed it. I said this to myself as
I **⓬**rocked. Mrs. Jelinek stood in **⓭**the hall doorway with her arms
15 folded, mostly looking out the front door. By now life **⓮**seemed

---

❶ stay right in the house: このまま家にとどまる
❷ under no condition: 何があっても（絶対〜しない）
❸ a plan I knew would work: 上手く行く（work）とわかっている計画。p. 12,
　　註**❼**を参照。
❹ will power: 意志の力
❺ go on keeping quiet: このまま静かにしている
❻ break the spell I was starting to work: いまかけようとしている呪いを破る
❼ concentrate: 集中する
❽ I was confident that ...: 〜だという確信があった
❾ force of character: 人格の力
❿ had fitted me for just such a battle: まさにこういう戦いに私をふさわしく
　　してくれていた（人格、教育からして私はこういう戦いに向いていた）

だ。彼女のところには電話があるのだ。姉が出ていったとき、あたしは顔も上げなかった。あたしは大きな決断をしたのだ。それはつまり、この家にとどまること、どんなことがあってもあそこに連れもどされたりはしないということだった。それが難しいことはわかってる。でもあたしには計画があった。じぶんの持っている意志の力をぜんぶつかえば、きっとうまく行くはずだ。あたしにはわかる。あたしの意志の力はすごく強いのだ。

　まず大事なのは、このまましばらく大人しくしていること。これからかけようとしている呪いを破るような言葉は、一言だって言っちゃいけない。精神をしっかり集中させることももちろん必要だが、それはあたしにとっては簡単なことだ。これはきっと、姉とあたしとの戦いになるだろう。でもあたしには自信があった。あたしの意志は強いのだし、教育だって姉より受けている。だからこういう戦いにはぴったりなのだ。勝つ自信はある。あたしはただひたすら、胸のうちで、こうなれ、こうなれ、と念じつづければいい。そうすればちゃんとあたしの意志どおりにことは起こるのだ。ロッキングチェアに揺られながらあたしはじぶんにそう言い聞かせた。ミセス・ジェリネクは廊下の玄関前に腕組みをして立ち、たいていは玄関ごしに外を見ていた。ひさしぶりに、すごくひさしぶりに、人生が明快な、目的にみちたもの

⓫ the way I willed it: 私が念じたとおりに
⓬ rock(ed): （ロッキングチェアを）揺らす
⓭ the hall doorway: 廊下の玄関口、玄関扉の前
⓮ seemed much clearer and more purposeful than ...: 〜よりずっと明快で、目的がはっきりしていると思えた

much clearer and more purposeful ❶than it had in a long, long time. This way I would have what I wanted. "No one can stop you," I thought.

It was a quarter of an hour before my sister came back. When she walked in she had both Mrs. Schultz and Mrs. Schultz's brother with her, and all three of them looked a little frightened. I knew exactly what had happened even before she told Mrs. Jelinek. She had called the Home and complained to Dr. Dunn that I had been ❷released, and he had been very much excited and told her to ❸hold on to me by all means because I had not been ❹discharged at all but had somehow *got out*. I was a little shocked ❺to hear it put that way, ❻but now that I thought of it, I had to admit to myself that that was just what I had done.

I got up when Mrs. Schultz's brother came in, and ❼glared at him hard.

"❽Take it easy, now, ❾Miss Ethel," he said, and his voice

---

❶ than it had in a long, long time: 人生がすごく長いあいだそうだった以上に。ものすごく久しぶりに、人生に明快さと目的が戻ってきたように感じられたということ。

❷ release(d): 〜を退院させる

❸ hold on to me by all means: 何としても私を逃がさない

❹ discharge(d): 〜を退院させる。ここでは前行の released とそんなに変わらないが、人質を解放するというときは release を使うし、兵士を除隊させるときは discharge を使う、と微妙な違いはある。

❺ to hear it put that way: そんな風に言われるのを聞いて。*Well, you can put it that way.*（まあ、そういう言い方もできますけどね）

❻ but now that I thought of it: しかし考えてみれば

❼ glare(d): 睨みつける

であるような気がした。これなら大丈夫、きっとあたしの望みどおりになる。「だれもあんたを止められやしない」とあたしはじぶんに言った。

　十五分たって、やっと姉が戻ってきた。姉はミセス・シュルツだけでなくその弟まで連れてきていた。三人ともすこしびくついているみたいだった。姉がミセス・ジェリネクに話すまえからあたしには事情が完璧に呑みこめた。姉は病院に電話をかけてドクター・ダンを呼びだし、なんだってあの子を退院させたりしたんです、と文句を言ったのだ。すると、すっかり興奮しているドクターは答える──いいですか、絶対逃がしちゃいけませんよ、退院させてなんかいないんですから、どうやってかは知らんが脱走したんです、あの子は、と。脱走、という言い方をされてあたしはちょっとショックだった。でもまあ考えてみれば認めないわけにはいかない。あたしはたしかに脱走したのだ。

　ミセス・シュルツの弟が入ってくるとあたしは立ちあがり、怖い顔で弟をにらみつけた。

「まあまあ落ちついて、ミス・エセル」と弟は不安そうな声で言った。あた

---

❽ Take it easy, now: まあ落ちつきなさい
❾ Miss Ethel: かつてはこのようにファーストネームにも Miss をつけた。

sounded nervous. I bowed low to him: at least he was polite.

"❶'Lo, Steve," said Mrs. Jelinek.

I watched every move they made. I would have died rather than let the spell be broken. I felt I could ❷hold it together only by
5 a great effort. Mrs. Schultz's brother was ❸scratching the side of his nose, and his other hand ❹twitched in his pants pocket. I knew he would give me no trouble. Mrs. Schultz and Mrs. Jelinek ❺would not go any further than my sister told them to. And she herself was terrified of me, ❻for although ❼I had never done her any harm, she
10 had always been convinced that some day I would. ❽It may be that she knew now ❾what I was about to do to her, but I doubt it, or she would have run away from the house.

"❿When they coming?" asked Mrs. Jelinek.

"⓫Soon's they can get here," said Mrs. Schultz.

15 They all stood in the doorway.

---

❶ 'Lo: hello
❷ hold it together only by a great effort: すごく頑張ることによってのみ、(呪いが) バラバラにならないよう保つ＝すごく頑張って、なんとか……保つ
❸ scratch(ing): 〜をぼりぼり掻く
❹ twitch(ed): ぴくぴく動く
❺ would not go any further than my sister told them to: 姉に命じられた以上には行かないだろう
❻ for: なぜなら〜
❼ I had never done her any harm: 私が彼女に危害を加えたことは一度もなかった
❽ It may be that ...: ひょっとすると〜ということかもしれない
❾ what I was about to do to her: 私が彼女にやろうとしていること

しは彼にむかって深々と御辞儀をした。すくなくともこの男は礼儀というものを心得ている。

「こんちは、スティーヴ」とミセス・ジェリネクが言った。

　あたしは連中の一挙一動を見まもった。ここで呪いを破ってしまうくらいなら死んだほうがましだ。ここはひとつよほど気を入れないと、とあたしは思った。ミセス・シュルツの弟は鼻の横をごりごり掻いている。もう一方の手はズボンのポケットのなかでもぞもぞ動いている。この男については面倒はあるまい。ミセス・シュルツとミセス・ジェリネクも姉に命じられた以上のことはしないだろう。それに姉にしたって、あたしのことを怖がっている。姉は昔からずっと信じていたのだ。いままでそんなことは一度もないけれど、いつかきっと、あたしに傷つけられる日が来るにちがいない、と。いまここで、もしかしたら姉は、あたしがなにをやろうとしているか、わかっていたかもしれない。でもたぶんそうじゃなかっただろう。もしわかっていたら、一目散に家から逃げだしていたはずだから。

「いつ迎えに来るの？」とミセス・ジェリネクがたずねた。

「できるだけ早く行きますって」とミセス・シュルツが言った。

　彼らはみんな玄関口に立っていた。

⑩ When they coming?: When are they coming?
⑪ Soon's: As soon as

"I see they rescued the flood victims, you remember last night on the radio?" said Mrs. Schultz's brother. He lit a cigarette and ❶leaned back against the banisters.

The house was very ugly, but I already was getting ideas for
5 making it look better. I ❷have excellent taste in decoration. I tried not to think of those things, and said over and over inside my head: "❸Make it work."

Mrs. Jelinek finally sat down on the couch by the door, pulled her skirt around her legs and coughed. She still looked red in the
10 face and serious. ❹I could have laughed out loud when I thought of what they were really waiting to see if they had only known it.

I heard a car door slam outside. I looked out. Two of the men from the Home were coming up the walk. Somebody else was ❺sitting at the wheel, waiting. My sister went quickly to the front
15 door and opened it. One of the men said: "Where is she?" They both came in and stood a second looking at me and grinning.

---

❶ leaned back against the banisters: 階段の手すりに寄りかかった
❷ have excellent taste in decoration: インテリアの素晴らしいセンスがある
❸ Make it work: うまく行かせろ。it はかけようとしている呪いを指す。
❹ I could have laughed out loud when I thought of ...: 〜を考えると、大声で笑ってしまいそうだった
❺ sitting at the wheel: 運転席に座っている。ハンドルのことは the (steering) wheel という。

「洪水の被害者たちは救出されたらしいですね。昨晩のラジオ、聞きました？」とミセス・シュルツの弟が言って、煙草に火をつけ、階段の手すりにもたれかかった。

　なんて醜い家だろう。でもあたしの頭のなかにはもう、どうやったらもっとましになるか、あれこれアイデアが浮かんできていた。あたしのインテリアの趣味は抜群なのだ。でも当座はそういうことはなるべく考えないようにして、頭のなかで何度も何度も「あたしの思いどおりになれ」とくり返した。

　しばらくして、ミセス・ジェリネクが玄関わきに置かれたソファに腰かけ、スカートを左右に引っぱって直し、えへんと咳払いをした。彼女の顔はあいかわらず赤く、真剣そうだった。あたしは思わずゲラゲラ笑いだしそうになった。これからどういうことになるのか、こいつらにもしわかったら、みんなどんな顔をするだろう？

　自動車のドアがばたんと閉まる音が表で聞こえた。あたしは外を見た。ホームの男が二人、家の前の道をこっちへやって来る。もう一人だれかが運転席にすわったまま待っている。姉が大急ぎで玄関に行って、ドアをあけた。片方の男が言った。「どこです？」。そして二人ともなかに入ってきて、しばし立ちどまってあたしを見つめ、にやっと笑った。

"Well, hel-*lo!*" said one. The other turned and said to my sister: "No trouble?" ❶She shook her head. "❷It's a wonder you couldn't be more careful," she said angrily. "❸They get out like that, ❹how do *you* know what they're going to do?"

5　　The man grunted and came over to me. "❺Wanna come with us? I know somebody who's waiting to see you."

　　I got up and walked slowly across the room, looking at the rug all the way, with one of the men ❻on each side of me. When I got to the doorway beside my sister I pulled my hand out of the pocket
10 of my coat and looked at it. I had one of my stones in my hand. It was very easy. Before either of them could stop me I ❼reached out and ❽stuffed the stone into her mouth. She screamed just before I touched her, and just afterward her lips were bleeding. But ❾the whole thing took a very long time. Everybody was standing
15 perfectly still. Next, the two men ❿had hold of my arms very tight and I was looking around the room at the walls. I felt that my front

---

❶ She shook her head: 首を横に振った。"No trouble?" に対する返答なので、同意を示す。

❷ It's a wonder you couldn't be more careful: あなた方がもっと注意深くやれないのは驚きだ＝もうちょっと気をつけてよね

❸ They get out like that: If they get out like that（こんなに簡単に脱走するようでは）

❹ how do *you* know what they're going to do?: 彼らが何をするか、どうやってあなた方にわかるのか＝何をしでかすか、わかりようがないじゃないか

❺ Wanna come with us?: Do you want to come with us?

❻ on each side of me: 私の左右に

❼ reached out: 手を伸ばした

❽ stuff(ed): ～を詰め込む、押し込む

「やあやあ、こんにちは！」と片方が言った。もう一方が姉のほうをむいて、「なにか厄介なことは？」と言った。姉は首を横に振った。「もうちょっと気をつけて下さってもいいんじゃないかしら」と姉は怒った声で言った。「こんなふうにやすやす脱走できちゃうなんて、なにをしでかすか、わかったもんじゃないわ」

　男はなにかぶつぶつ呟いて、あたしに近よってきた。「俺たちといっしょに来ないか？　君に会いたがってる人がいるんだよ」

　あたしは立ちあがり、二人の男にはさまれて、目を足もとのじゅうたんに釘づけにしたまま、ゆっくりと部屋を横ぎっていった。玄関口にたどり着き、姉の横まで来ると、あたしはコートのポケットに入れた手を出し、それをながめた。手のなかには例の石が一つ入っている。すごく簡単だった。二人の男が止める間もなく、あたしは手をのばして姉の口のなかに石をつっ込んだ。あたしが姉に触れる直前、姉は悲鳴をあげた。その直後には、姉の口から血が流れていた。でもずいぶん長い時間がかかった。みんなじっと、ぴくりとも動かずに立ちつくしていた。と、二人の男があたしの腕をしっかり押さえていた。あたしは部屋の壁を見まわしていた。あたしの前歯が折れてい

❾ the whole thing took a very long time: 始めから終わりまで、ものすごく時間がかかった
❿ had hold of my arms very tight: 私の腕をしっかり摑んだ

teeth were broken. I could taste blood on my lips. I thought I was going to **❶**faint. I wanted to put my hand to my mouth, but they held my arms. "This is the turning point," I thought.

I shut my eyes very hard. When I opened them everything was
5 different and I knew I had won. For a moment I could not see very clearly, but even during that moment I saw myself sitting on **❷**the divan with my hands in front of my mouth. **❸**As my vision cleared, I saw that the men were holding my sister's arms, and that she **❹**was putting up a terrific struggle. I buried my face in my hands and
10 did not look up again. While they **❺**were getting her out the front door, they **❻**managed to knock over the umbrella stand and smash it. It hurt her **❼**ankle and she kicked pieces of **❽**porcelain back into the hall. I was delighted. They dragged her along the walk to the car, and one man sat on each side of her in the back. She was
15 yelling and showing her teeth, but as they left **❾**the city limits she stopped, and began to cry. All the same, she was really counting

---

❶ faint: 気を失う

❷ the divan: 背もたれのないソファ

❸ As my vision cleared: 視界がはっきりしてくるにつれて

❹ was putting up a terrific struggle: 激しく抵抗していた。put up のあとに a fight やその類語が来る言い方。

❺ were getting her out the front door: 彼女を玄関の外に出そうとしていた

❻ managed to knock over the umbrella stand and smash it: (うっかり、よりによって) 傘立てをひっくり返して割った

❼ (an) ankle: 足首、くるぶし

❽ porcelain: 磁器

❾ the city limits: 市境

Paul Bowles

るのがわかった。唇は血の味がした。失神しそうだ、とあたしは思った。あたしは片手を口へ持っていきたかったけど、男たちはあたしの腕を押さえつけていた。「ここがわかれ目だ」とあたしは思った。

　あたしはぎゅっと眼をつぶった。眼をあけると、なにもかもが変わっていた。あたしは勝ったのだ。はじめの一瞬はまだ、いまひとつはっきりと見えなかったけれど、その瞬間でさえあたしには、長椅子にすわって両手を口に当てているじぶんの姿が見えた。視界がだんだんはっきりしてくると、男たちが姉の両腕を押さえているのが見えた。姉はすさまじい勢いで抵抗していた。あたしは顔を両手にうずめ、そのまま顔を上げなかった。連中は彼女を玄関の外に連れだそうとして、ついでに傘立てをひっくり返して割ってしまった。磁器が彼女のくるぶしをしたたか打った。彼女は足をばたばたさせて、破片を廊下側に蹴りかえした。あたしは愉快だった。男たちは彼女を自動車まで引きずっていき、彼女を両側からはさんだまま後部席に乗りこんだ。彼女は歯をむき出しにしてわめいていた。でも町はずれに出たあたりでわめくのをやめ、こんどは泣き出した。それでも彼女はちゃんと、ホームへ

the service stations along the road on the way back to the Home, and she found there was one more of them than she had thought. When they came to ❶the grade crossing near the spot where the train accident had happened, she looked out, but the car ❷was over
⁵ the track before she realized she was looking out the wrong side.

Driving in through the gate, she really ❸broke down. They kept promising her ice cream for dinner, but she ❹knew better than to believe them. As she walked through the main door between the two men she stopped on ❺the threshold, took out one of the
¹⁰ stones from her coat pocket and put it into her mouth. She tried to swallow it, but it choked her, and they ❻rushed her down the hall into a little waiting room and made her give it up. The strange thing, now that I think about it, was that no one realized she was not I.

¹⁵ They put her to bed, and by morning she no longer felt like crying: she was too tired.

---

❶ the grade crossing: 踏切
❷ was over the track: 線路を越えた
❸ broke down <break down: (苦しみに耐えきれず) 泣き崩れる、取り乱す
❹ knew better than to believe them: 彼らの言うことを信じるほど馬鹿ではなかった。p. 34, l. 16 の knew enough not to とほぼ同じ。
❺ the threshold: 敷居
❻ rushed her down the hall: 引っ立てるように廊下を先へ行かせた

戻るまでの道すがら、ガソリンスタンドの数をかぞえていて、それはじぶん
が思っていたより一つ多かった。列車事故が起きたそばの踏切に来ると、彼
女は外を見た。が、じぶんが反対側を見ていることに気づいたときには、車
はもう線路をこえていた。

　車が門を抜けてなかへ入ったところで、彼女は本気で取り乱した。夕ごは
んにアイスクリームをあげるからね、と連中は何度も約束したけれど、彼女
だってそれを本気にするほど馬鹿じゃなかった。二人の男にはさまれて表玄
関のドアまで来ると、敷居のところで立ちどまり、コートのポケットから石
を一つ取り出して、それを口のなかに入れた。彼女はそれを飲みこもうとし
たが、喉につっかえて息がつまってしまった。男たちは大あわてで彼女を小
さな待合室まで引っぱっていき、石を吐きださせた。いまになって思うとす
ごく不思議なのだけど、彼女があたしじゃないことに、だれも気がつかな
かったのだ。

　連中は彼女をベッドに寝かしつけた。朝になると彼女は泣く気もなくなっ
ていた。もう疲れきってしまっていたのだ。

It's the middle of the afternoon and **❶**raining torrents. She is sitting on her bed (the very one I used to have) in the Home, **❷**writing all this down on paper. She never would have thought of doing that **❸**up until yesterday, but now she thinks she has become
5 me, and so she does everything I used to do.

The house is very quiet. I am still in the living room, sitting on the divan. I could walk upstairs and look into her bedroom if I wanted to. But it is such a long time since I have been up there, and I no longer know how the rooms are arranged. So I prefer to stay
10 down here. If I look up I can see **❹**the square window of colored glass over the stairs. Purple and orange, **❺**an hourglass design, **❻**only the light never comes in very much because the house next door is so close. Besides, the rain is coming down hard here, too.

15

---

❶ raining torrents: 土砂降りの雨が降っていて
❷ writing all this down: こうしたいっさいを書き留めて
❸ up until yesterday: 昨日までは。up が入ることで意味が強まる。
❹ the square window of colored glass over the stairs: 階段の上の、色つきガラスが入った四角い窓
❺ an hourglass design: 砂時計の模様
❻ only: ただし。p. 40, l. 16 に同じ。

　いまは午後のなかばごろ、どしゃぶりの雨が降っている。彼女はホームでベッドの上に腰かけて（あたしが使っていたベッドだ）、いっさいの出来事を紙に書きとめている。そんなことをやってみようなんて、昨日までは夢にも思わなかったろう。でも彼女はもう、じぶんがあたしになったと思っている。だからあたしがいつもやっていたことをぜんぶやろうとするのだ。

　家のなかはとても静かだ。あたしはまだ居間にいて、長椅子に腰かけている。その気になれば、階段を上がって彼女の寝室をのぞくこともできる。でもずいぶん長いこと二階には行っていないし、部屋の配置がどうなっているのかもあたしは知らない。だからとりあえずはもうしばらくここにいようと思う。顔を上げると、階段の上に、色つきガラスの四角い窓が見える。紫色とオレンジ色、砂時計の模様。でも日光はそんなに入ってこない。となりの家がぴったりくっついているからだ。それにだいいち、ここでもやっぱり雨は激しく降っているのだ。

ちなみに

　この短篇はサラ・ドライバー（Sara Driver）によって 1981 年に映画化されている。静かで緊迫感のある 48 分の作品であり、おおむね原作を忠実に追っているが、語り手と姉が入れ替わったあとの処理が興味深い。脚本はドライバーと、彼女のパートナー、ジム・ジャームッシュ（当時はまだ『ストレンジャー・ザン・パラダイス』で鮮烈デビューを果たす前）の共同執筆で、撮影もジャームッシュ。

A Vision
Rebecca Brown

A Vision

レベッカ・ブラウン

難易度 2
★ ★ ☆

レベッカ・ブラウン
（Rebecca Brown, 1956- ）

呪文のようにシンプルで、反復を効果的に使った文章を特徴とし、実験的要素の強いレズビアン小説（代表作 *Annie Oakley's Girl*, 1993）や、エイズで死んでいく友人たちを介護した体験に基づく静かな作品（*The Gifts of the Body*, 1995）などをこれまでに発表してきた。

W[hen] I was six my family moved to Spain. My father was [1]in the military and though my mother had not been happy with the [2]peripatetic life our family led, she was excited about this [3]posting. This posting would let her go to Europe and take
5 her daughters, my older sister and me, to museums and historic homes and castles. My brother wasn't interested in any of that. Like my father, he preferred fishing. But "the girls," as my father and brother called Mom and us, loved going to museums. My sister, who wanted to be an artist, liked looking at the paintings. I
10 liked looking at the [4]armor. I loved those huge tall statues of silver and bronze, with their shiny [5]shins and [6]pointy, [7]sectioned feet that looked like armadillos. I liked the [8]plush [9]royal blue and purple [10]brocade and quilted cloth and [11]chain mail. I liked looking at the [12]face guards with slits and wondering what it looked like
15 inside. I loved the [13]plumes on helmets, the gold [14]carved handles of swords. I loved [15]the red-and-white striped and blue-and-gold

A Vision: タイトルをしいて訳すなら「幻視」が一番近いだろうし、本文中の vision はひとまずそう訳した。が、本当は「幻」というよりもっとリアルなものを示唆しているので、できれば避けたい。「見えるもの」「見えてくるもの」というふうに訳すのも一案かもしれないが、ここではあえて原語を残し、まずは読者に「何だろう」と思ってもらうように仕向けた。

[1] in the military: 軍隊に勤務して
[2] peripatetic: 渡り歩きの
[3] posting: (特に軍隊の) 任命、配属
[4] armor: よろいかぶと
[5] shin(s): 向こうずね
[6] pointy: 先の尖った
[7] sectioned feet that looked like armadillos: アルマジロのように、いくつも

　私が六才のとき家族はスペインに移り住んだ。父が軍隊に勤務していて、それまでの引越しつづきの暮らしを母は喜んでいなかったけれど、今度の転任については楽しみにしていた。今度はヨーロッパに行けるのだし、娘たち（姉と私）を美術館や由緒ある屋敷やお城に連れていくこともできる。私の兄はそういうことには全然興味がなかった。父と同じで、釣りの方がいいと兄は言った。でも父と兄言うところの「女性軍」、つまり母と私たち姉妹は美術館や博物館に行くのが大好きだった。姉は画家になるのが夢で、絵を見るのも好きだった。私は鎧甲（よろいかぶと）を見るのが好きだった。ぴかぴかの脛当てがついて、足はアルマジロみたいに尖って細かく分かれている、巨大で背の高い、銀色と青銅色の像が大好きだった。紺青色や紫色のビロード製ブロケードや、キルトの布や、鎖かたびらも大好きだった。細い切れ目の入った面を見て、中はどうなっているんだろうと考えるのも好きだった。甲（かぶと）についた羽飾り、彫刻の入った金色の剣の柄（つか）も大好き、馬の像に着せた赤白のストライプや青と金のチェックの垂れ布も大好き、次々に出会う昔の物語も大好き。

❽ plush: フラシ天の。ビロードの一種で、「豪華」というイメージがある。
❾ royal blue and purple: royal blue は名前からして高貴な響きがあるし、purple も伝統的に高貴さとつながることの多い色。
❿ brocade: 金襴
⓫ chain mail: 鎖かたびら
⓬ face guard(s): 顔覆い、面
⓭ plume(s): 羽飾り
⓮ carved handles: 彫刻を施した柄（つか）
⓯ the red-and-white striped and blue-and-gold checked skirts: 垂れ布（skirts）のうちいくつかは赤白の縞模様で、いくつかは青と金の格子模様だということ。

checked skirts the statues of the horses wore. I loved the stories I was learning about ❶ the olden days. I decided that I wanted to be ❷ a knight.

My best friend was our neighbor, Chuckie Thom. Chuckie and
5 I would get ❸ ratty old bath towels from our mothers and draw ❹ insignias on them with magic markers—dragons or castles or lions or ❺ gargoyles—and ❻ safety-pin them around our necks ❼ so they'd hang down our backs like capes. Then we'd run around waving our ❽ rulers or our big brothers' baseball bats as if they
10 were swords and yell, ❾ "But my Lord, I am not worthy! I am not worthy!" while we ❿ stabbed out ⓫ the innards and ⓬ chopped off the heads of our ⓭ imaginary ⓮ foes. We'd ⓯ turn garbage-can lids into shields and our fathers' ⓰ pool cues into ⓱ lances and ⓲ joust or ⓳ go on a mission to find my brother's baseball trophy, the Holy
15 Grail.

---

❶ the olden days: olden はたいてい、そのあとに days か times が来る。「遠い昔」と言いたいときには the old days よりこちらの方がふさわしいことも多い。

❷ a knight: 騎士

❸ ratty: 薄汚い

❹ insignia(s): 記章。そのあとの dragons or castles ... といった具体例から見て、紋章のたぐいが想定されているようである。

❺ gargoyle(s): ゴシック建築で、怪物をかたどった水落とし口のこと。

❻ safety-pin: ここでは動詞。「〜を安全ピンで留める」

❼ so they'd hang down our backs like capes: ケープのように背中に垂れるよう。so they'd (=they would) ... は p. 30, l. 5 と同じく「〜するように」の意。

❽ ruler(s): 定規

❾ "But my Lord, I am not worthy! I am not worthy!": 特に「出典」があるわけではなく、子供がいかにも中世っぽいフレーズを捏造している感じ。

大きくなったら騎士になろう、と私は決めた。

　私の一番の仲よしは近所に住んでいるチャッキー・トムだった。チャッキーと二人でそれぞれ母親から使い古しのバスタオルをもらって、マジックで紋章を描いて——竜、城、獅子、ガーゴイル——首に巻いて安全ピンで止め、ケープみたいに背中に垂らす。それから二人で、定規か、兄たちの野球のバットを剣のように振り回しながら駆け回り、「ですがご主人様、わたくしめは卑しき者にございます！　卑しき者にございます！」とわめきながら、想像の敵の内臓をえぐり出し、首を切り落とした。ゴミバケツの蓋を盾に変え、父親のビリヤードのキューを槍に変えて一騎打ちをしたり、聖杯を、すなわち私の兄の野球トロフィーを探す任を帯びて旅に出たりした。

❿ stab(bed) out ...: 〜をえぐり出す

⓫ the innards: 内臓

⓬ chop(ped) off ...: 〜をちょん切る

⓭ imaginary: 想像上の

⓮ foe(s): 敵。enemy より古めかしい。

⓯ turn garbage-can lids into shields: ごみバケツのふたを盾に変える

⓰ pool cue(s): ビリヤードのキュー

⓱ lance(s): 槍

⓲ joust: 馬上槍試合をする。騎士道物語でのみお目にかかる気がする語。

⓳ go on a mission to find ... the Holy Grail: 聖杯を見つける任を帯びて旅に出る。聖杯探求は、貴婦人への愛と並んで、騎士道物語の大きな要素。

Most often Chuck was ❶King Arthur, but he also got to be
❷Edward the Black Prince, Henry the Fifth, or Richard the Lion-
Hearted. He had a choice. I, because I was a girl, was always
❸Joan of Arc. ❹Except for how she was burned at the stake and her
5 religion, which I didn't understand, I liked Joan of Arc, so mostly I
liked being her.

Sometimes, when Chuck had been called home for dinner and
I played late alone, I would imagine things. I would get very, very
quiet, then I would lift my arms straight up toward the sky, close
10 my eyes, and ❺tip my head so far back ❻I would get dizzy. Then I
would wait. I waited until I could almost ❼feel against my skin, or
at least in the air above my skin, a touch. Or if not exactly a touch,
at least ❽the passing of something through the air beside me, ❾a
spirit or someone right next, or at least, near to me. I waited until,
15 although, because my eyes were closed I couldn't see, I could,
almost, or so it seemed, see something like ❿a figure, like a ghost, a

❶ King Arthur: 騎士道物語においてもっとも有名な人物の一人。6世紀ごろの伝
　説的なブリトン人の王。
❷ Edward the Black Prince, Henry the Fifth ...: 三人とも中世に実在した王だ
　が、20世紀なかばのアメリカの子供たちからすれば十分伝説的存在。
❸ Joan of Arc: ジャンヌ・ダルク（Jeanne d'Arc）
❹ Except for how she was burned at the stake and her religion, which I
　didn't understand: "how she was burned at the stake" と "her religion,
　which I didn't understand" が同格で、Except for A and B（AとBを除け
　ば）という形になっている。「火あぶりにされたことと、私には理解できない彼
　女の宗教とを別にすれば」。the stake: 火刑柱
❺ tip my head so far back: 首をすごくうしろに傾ける
❻ I would get dizzy: that I would get dizzy. "so ... that ..." （大変〜なので〜

　チャックはアーサー王になることが一番多かったけれど、エドワード黒太子、ヘンリー五世、リチャード獅子心王になったりもした。チャックには選ぶ余地があったのだ。私は女の子だったからいつもジャンヌ・ダルクだった。火あぶりにされることと、よくわからない宗教を信じていること以外はジャンヌ・ダルクが好きだったから、彼女になるのもまあ嫌じゃなかった。

　時おり、チャックが夕ご飯だと言われて家に帰り、一人で遅くまで遊ぶとき、私はいろんなことを想像した。すごく、すごく静かにしていて、それから両腕をまっすぐ空に向けて上げ、目を閉じて首をぐっとうしろに、めまいがするくらいうしろに傾ける。そうして待つ。肌に、少なくとも肌の上あたりの空気に何かが触れるのがほとんど感じられるまで待つ。触れるとまでは行かないにしても、少なくともそばの空気に何かが、何かの霊か人間かが、私のすぐ横を、少なくとも近くを通っていく感じ。目を閉じているから何も見えないのだけれど、ぎゅっとつむった目の奥に何かが——何か人影のような幽霊のような形か色のようなものがほとんど見えてくるまで、見えてくる

である）の that は口語ではよく省略される。
❼ feel against my skin ... a touch: 肌に何かが触れるのを感じる
❽ the passing of something through the air: 何かが空気中を通り過ぎていくこと
❾ a spirit: 霊
❿ a figure: 人の姿

shape, or colors, inside my tight-shut eyes. I waited until I almost heard, not in my ears, but in my head, a sound like someone saying something, whispering, as if someone was telling me a secret. I stayed like that, my head tipped back, my eyes shut tight
5 and ❶waited for, like Joan of Arc, a vision.

When we ❷moved back to the states it was to Texas, where we had never lived before. The next year I entered sixth grade. All of the teachers at Stephen F. Austin Elementary School, home of
10 ❸the Fighting Rams, except the football coach who was also ❹the principal, were women. All of the women teachers, except one, ❺dressed up for school. ❻Mrs. Kreidler, my homeroom teacher, never wore the same dress twice and her shoes always matched her ❼dress. Once she brought a record to class and sang to us in
15 her high thin voice, a song about the mountains. The dress she wore that day had ❽a pattern of mountains and stars. Miss Bryant, the art and music teacher, wore pink or other ❾pastel, usually suits

---

❶ waited for, like Joan of Arc, a vision: ジャンヌ・ダルクみたいにヴィジョンが訪れるのを待った。ジャンヌ・ダルクといえば少女のときに神の声を聞き天使の姿を見たということになっている。

❷ moved back to the states: またアメリカに戻った。アメリカ人が国外で「アメリカ」と言うとき一番一般的なのがこの the states（または the States）という言い方。

❸ the Fighting Rams:「戦う雄羊」という名前を見ただけで、たぶん大半の人はフットボール・チームのことだろうと見当がつく。

❹ the principal: 校長

❺ dressed up for school: めかし込んで学校に来た

❻ Mrs. Kreidler, my homeroom teacher: 私の担任のクライドラー先生。小中高では「先生」に当たる言葉は Teacher ではなく Mrs., Miss, Mr. である。

気がするまで、私は待った。音がほとんど聞こえてくるまで私は待った、耳にではなく頭のなかで、誰かが何か言っているような、ささやいているような、誰かが私に何か秘密を告げているような音が聞こえてくるまで待った。そんなふうにじっと、首をうしろに傾けて、目をぎゅっと閉じて、ジャンヌ・ダルクのように幻視が訪れるのを待った。

一家でアメリカに戻ってくると、今度はテキサスに移った。テキサスに住むのは初めてだった。その翌年、私は6年生になった。「ファイティング・ラムズ」を擁するスティーヴン・F・オースティン校の先生たちは、フットボール・コーチを兼ねている校長先生以外みんな女だった。一人を例外として、女の先生はみんな着飾って学校に来た。私の担任のミセス・クライドラーは絶対に同じワンピースを二度着てこなかったし、靴も必ずワンピースに合わせていた。ある日先生は学校にレコードを持ってきて、高く細い声で自分も歌って私たちに聞かせた。山についての歌だった。その日先生が着ていたワンピースには山と星の模様が入っていた。美術と音楽のミス・ブライアントはピンクなどのパステルカラーの、たいていは肩の張ったスーツを着てきた。先生が廊下を歩くと教室の隅々まで香水が匂ってきた。理科のミセス・

❼ (a) dress: 日本語の「ドレス」のみならず「ワンピース」も含む。
❽ a pattern: 模様
❾ pastel: パステルカラー

with big shoulders and you could smell her perfume all the way inside the room ❶where she walked in the hall. Mrs. Grant, the science teacher, was old and wore lots of powder and had bright, red, perfectly round circles on her cheeks and lots of shiny rings on
5 her ❷knobby hands. Sometimes she ❸tripped on her heels.

Miss Hopkins, however, was different. She had short, straight black hair that she never ❹curled and you could see that it was shaved ❺at the back of her neck. She always wore ❻penny loafers or ❼flats, never heels. Her clothes were ❽plain, black or gray or
10 navy ❾A-line skirts with light blue or white or beige open-collared shirts. She never wore dresses and never patterns or pastels. Her glasses did not have ❿cats'-eye frames or pointy frames or frames held on with a gold-looking chain the way the other teachers did. Her frames were plain and black. She taught us math.
15 The first day of class Miss Hopkins told us that our ⓫grades would be ⓬based "strictly on class average," of all our homework

---

❶ where she walked in the hall: 彼女が廊下を歩いたところでは
❷ knobby: 節くれだった
❸ trip(ped): つまずく
❹ curl(ed): 〜にカールをかける
❺ at the back of her neck: うなじのところで
❻ penny loafers: 靴紐を結ぶ必要のない、普通のカジュアルな革靴。
❼ flats: ヒールのない靴
❽ plain: 無地の、地味な
❾ A-line: A字形の。上が締まっていて下がゆるやかに広がっている服を言う。
❿ cats'-eye frames: 猫の目を思わせる、両端がつり上がった眼鏡フレーム。いかにも女性的という感じがする。次の pointy frames は端がさらに尖っている。
⓫ grade(s): 成績

グラントは歳をとっていて白粉をたっぷりはたき、頬には明るい赤の、完璧
に丸い円を描いていた。骨ばった両手にはぴかぴかの指輪をたくさんつけて
いた。先生はときどきヒールを引っかけてつまずいた。

　けれどミス・ホプキンズは違っていた。短いまっすぐの黒髪にカールをか
けたりはしなかったし、うなじは剃刀で剃ってあるのが見えた。履いている
のはいつもコインローファーかフラットシューズで、ハイヒールは絶対に履
かなかった。服は無地で、黒かグレーかネイビーのＡラインスカート、それ
に水色か白かベージュのオープンカラーのシャツ。ワンピースは一度も着て
こなかったし、柄のある服やパステルカラーも着なかった。眼鏡も、ほかの
先生たちみたいにキャッツアイフレームや尖ったフレームや金みたいな鎖で
止めたフレームではなかった。地味な黒のフレームだった。先生は算数を教
えていた。

　学期最初の日にミス・ホプキンズは、成績は「厳密に点数に基づいて」つ
けると言った。すべては宿題とテストの点数で決まる。ボーナス点はいっさ

⓬ based "strictly on class average":「厳密にクラスでの平均点に」基づいて。
　点数以外の主観的要素は入れないということ。

and tests. Miss Hopkins did not ❶give extra credit. ❷There was no arguing, no ❸Mickey-Mousing with Miss Hopkins. Everyone was afraid of her. Nobody ❹misbehaved with her. Not even the football players or the cheerleaders.

5   This was different from other classes. Football was ❺a huge, huge deal in our small Texas town. Football boys ❻were let out of class to practice. Some of the teachers ❼flirted with them, or with their dads, or ❽looked the other way when the football boys ❾copied from the smart kids during tests. Some teachers had been known to ❿hold some big boys back a grade ⓫so they would be even bigger and play even harder the next year. Miss Hopkins, however, ⓬did none of that. She treated the football boys and cheerleader girls like anybody else. She treated everyone the same. ⓭She had no pets.

15   Every fall there were cheerleader ⓮tryouts and for the weeks before the tryouts our ⓯gym periods were ⓰devoted to learning

---

❶ give extra credit: 余分に点数を与える。点数以外の、たとえば「フットボール・チームのレギュラーだから」といった理由で、ということ。

❷ There was no arguing: 文句を言っても無駄だった

❸ Mickey-Mousing: 可愛く、悪戯っぽくふるまう感じ。

❹ misbehave(d): 不作法にふるまう

❺ a huge, huge deal: とてもとても重要なこと。a big deal という言い方は非常によく使われ、ここではそれをずっと強調した言い方にしている（ここもそうだが、皮肉を込めることも少なくない）。

❻ were let out of class to practice: 練習するために授業から出してもらえた＝授業を免除された

❼ flirt(ed): 日本語にしにくい語だが、異性に対し思わせぶりな言葉を口にしたり、意味ありげに微笑んでみせたり、それとなく相手に触れたり、といったふるま

いなし。先生に文句を言ったり甘えたりしても無駄だった。誰もがホプキンズ先生を怖がっていた。先生相手に生意気にふるまう生徒はいなかった。フットボール選手やチアリーダーでも同じだった。

　その点、ほかの授業とは大違いだった。このテキサスの小さな町では、フットボールはすごく、すごく大事なことだった。フットボール部の男の子たちは練習のために授業も休めた。部の男の子といちゃつく先生も、男の子の父親といちゃつく先生もいたし、テストでフットボール部の子が勉強のできる子の答案を写しても見て見ぬふりをする先生もいた。体の大きい子が翌年もっと大きくなってもっと強力なプレーヤーになれるようわざと一年落第させた、などと噂される先生たちもいた。でもミス・ホプキンズはそういうことはいっさいしなかった。フットボール部の男の子も、チアリーダーの女の子も、ほかのみんなと同じに扱った。全員をみな同じに扱った。先生は誰もひいきにしなかった。

　毎年秋にチアリーダーの採用テストがあって、テストの前の何週間かは体育の時間ももっぱらチアの練習をやった。外の運動場に出て、チアの練習を

いをすること。

❽ looked the other way: 見ないふりをした

❾ copied from the smart kids: 頭のいい子の答案を写した

❿ hold ... back a grade: 〜を一年落第させる

⓫ so they would be ...: 彼らが〜であるように。p. 68, ll. 7-8 と同じ。

⓬ did none of that: そういうことは全然やらなかった

⓭ She had no pets: 誰もえこひいきしなかった。教師にえこひいきされる生徒のことを teacher's pet という。

⓮ tryout(s): テスト、選抜

⓯ gym period(s): 体育の時間

⓰ devoted: devote A to B で「A を B に充てる」。

cheers. We'd have class on the playfield outside where, instead of doing softball or ❶track or even ❷exercises, we did cheers.

I hated cheers. I was bad at them and ❸couldn't get my hand claps and my jumps and arm flaps to coordinate. I couldn't do
5 the ❹splits and I hated the leg kicks that you were supposed to do ❺in a line like the can-can. ❻I hated the way you were supposed to ❼wiggle your butt and smile and ❽squeal and yell ❾that high stupid way. But ❿it was class so I had to do it.

Most of the girls, ⓫the Brendas and RaeAnns and Darleens, the
10 cute ones, liked ⓬working on cheers and were looking forward to the tryouts. These were the girls who had a chance. But there were also the other girls. Girls with names like ⓭Carmen or Maria or Rosa, girls ⓮with the wrong religion because they were Catholic. Or girls who were fat or ⓯smelly, or wore dirty, old-fashioned
15 clothes. Girls who only lived there for a while before they had to

---

❶ track: 陸上競技

❷ exercise(s): 運動、体操

❸ couldn't get ... to coordinate: 〜をコーディネートできなかった、合わせられなかった

❹ split(s): スプリット（一直線に両脚を広げて床に座る演技）

❺ in a line like the can-can: カンカン踊りみたいに一列に並んで

❻ I hated the way you were supposed to ...: 〜することになっているのが嫌だった

❼ wiggle your butt: お尻を振る

❽ squeal: キーキー声を上げる

❾ that high stupid way: あの甲高い馬鹿みたいなやり方で

❿ it was class so I had to do it: 授業だからやらざるをえなかった

するのが授業なのだ。ソフトボールでもなく陸上でもなく体操ですらなく、みんなでチアをやる。

　私はチアが大嫌いだった。下手だったし、ハンドクラップとジャンプとアームフラップのタイミングも合わせられなかった。スプリットもできないし、一列に並んでカンカンみたいにやるレッグキックも大嫌いだった。お尻を振ってニコニコ笑ってキャーキャーわめいて馬鹿みたいな甲高い金切り声を上げなくちゃいけないのは嫌だった。でも授業だからやるしかなかった。

　たいていの女の子は、ブレンダとかレイアンとかダーリーンとかいった名前のキュートな女の子は、チアをやるのが好きだったし採用テストも楽しみにしていた。こういう子たちにはチャンスがあるのだ。でもそうじゃない子もいた。名前がカーメンとかマリーアとかローザとか、宗教もプロテスタントではなくカトリックの女の子たち。それと、太っていたり体臭があったり、汚い時代遅れの服を着ている子たち。この町にしばらく住んだらまた出てい

❶ the Brendas and RaeAnns and Darleens: 南部の白人労働階級の家の娘たち、という響き。

⓬ work(ing) on cheers: チアの練習をする

⓭ Carmen or Maria or Rosa: いかにもラテン系に響く名前。

⓮ with the wrong religion because they were Catholic: カトリックだから宗教も「間違っている」。たとえば 1920 年代の白人至上主義集団 Ku Klux Klan は黒人のみならずユダヤ人やカトリックにも敵意を抱いていた。1961 年、ケネディが大統領になったのは初のカトリック系大統領という意味でも画期的だった。

⓯ smelly: 臭（くさ）い

move again. There was one girl with **❶**a limp and one girl who had
❷peed at a Girl Scout meeting once and one **❸**retarded girl. These
were the girls who did not have a chance.

I didn't have a chance either, but not because I was Mexican-
5 American or poor or fat. I didn't have a chance, because I didn't
want to. I didn't want to be a cheerleader. I didn't want to wear the
little skirts they did and worry—or hope—that the boys would see
my underpants when I jumped up. I didn't want to **❹**go out with
boys and I didn't want to act the way girls did when they were
10 around them. I was the only girl in my sixth-grade class who did
not try out for cheerleader.

By the time I went to college, in 1975, very far away from Texas,
I wrote poetry, listened to **❺**cool music, ate vegetarian, had sex
15 with boys and girls my own age, and told stories. It was fun to tell
my **❻**artsy, liberal, drunken, feminist young friends stories about

---

❶ a limp: 足の不自由
❷ pee(d): おしっこをする
❸ retarded: 知能の発育が遅れた
❹ go out with ...: ～とデートする
❺ cool: かっこいい、イケてる
❻ artsy: 芸術家ふうの

くことになる女の子たち。足の悪い子、一度ガールスカウトの集会でおしっこを漏らした子、知的障害の子も一人ずついた。こういうのはみんなチャンスのない子たちだ。

　私だってチャンスはなかった。でもそれはメキシコ系だからでも貧乏だからでも太っているからでもなかった。私にチャンスがなかったのはチャンスなんか欲しくなかったからだ。私はチアリーダーになんかなりたくなかった。チアリーダーたちがはいている、ジャンプすると男の子たちにパンツを見られるんじゃないかとみんな心配する――あるいは期待する――短いスカートなんかはきたくなかった。男の子とデートなんかしたくなかったし、ほかの女の子たちが男の子が周りにいるところでふるまうみたいにふるまいたくなんかなかった。チアリーダーの採用テストを受けなかった6年生は私一人だった。

　一九七五年、テキサスからずっと遠くの大学に入ったころには、私は詩を書いて、クールな音楽を聴いて、ベジタリアンの食事をして、同世代の男と女両方とセックスをして、物語を語るようになっていた。アートっぽくてリベラルで酒びたりでフェミニストの若い友人たちにテキサスの物語を語るの

Texas. I **❶**shaped the story of my not trying out for cheerleader as a mock heroic tale of escape from **❷**an oppressive, southern-style femininity. Though I was a white girl who **❸**got to go to college, I **❹**allied myself in my **❺**retelling, with the Mexican girls and fat,
5 poor girls who **❻**couldn't get away the way I did. I **❼**attributed to myself **❽**a sassy rebelliousness that I had never actually had as a kid. In fact I was **❾**self-conscious and **❿**any rebelling I ever did I only did in private.

A lot of my life occurred in private, more and more of it as I
10 **⓫**slipped away from childhood and toward **⓬**whatever difficult thing was coming next. More and more I imagined things. I often did not understand them or admit them to myself and I certainly never told them to anyone else. But I imagined some things **⓭**so earnestly, so hopefully and longingly, that in my mind, I think, I
15 almost saw them.

*

❶ shaped the story of ... as a mock heroic tale: 〜の物語を擬似英雄譚として形作った。mock-heroic はたとえば、荘厳な叙事詩の文体で飲み屋の喧嘩を描写するといったような書き方をいう。
❷ an oppressive, southern-style femininity: 抑圧的な、南部風の女らしさ
❸ got to go to college: 大学に行かせてもらえた
❹ allied myself with ...: 〜と同盟を組んだ
❺ retelling: 語り直し
❻ couldn't get away the way I did: 私が逃げたようには逃げられなかった
❼ attributed to myself ...: 自分に〜の性質を与えた
❽ a sassy rebelliousness: 生意気な反抗心
❾ self-conscious: 自意識過剰の、のびのびふるまえない
❿ any rebelling I ever did I only did in private: ... I ever did / I only did ...と

は面白かった。チアリーダーのテストを受けなかった話を、私はコミカルな英雄譚に、抑圧的な南部流の女らしさからの逃走物語に仕立て上げた。私は白人で、大学にも行けたけれど、そうやって語り直した話のなかでは自分を、メキシコ系の子や太った貧乏な子、私みたいに逃げられはしない子たちと連帯させていた。実際に子供だったころには持てなかった小生意気な反抗心を私は自分に与えた。現実の私は自意識の強い、反抗するとしてもひっそり一人のときにしかできない子供だった。

　私の生活の中で、すごく多くのことがひっそり一人のときに起きていた。子供時代から少しずつ離れて、次にどんな困難が待っているにせよ先へ進んでいくにつれて、その度合いはますます増していった。私はますますいろんなことを想像するようになっていった。そうやって想像したことを、自分でも理解できないとき、認めたくないときもよくあったし、ましてや他人に打ちあけたりは絶対しなかった。けれど私は、時にすごくひたむきに、期待と願望を込めて想像したから、心のなかでは、そうやって想像したことがほとんど文字どおり見えていたんだと思う。

*

切る。「何か反抗をやるとしても、人のいないところでやった」。

❶ slipped away from childhood and toward ...: 幼年期から徐々に離れて、〜へ進んでいった

❷ whatever difficult thing was coming next: 次にやって来る、どんなものかはわからないけれどとにかく困難なこと

❸ so earnestly, so hopefully and longingly: 心底ひたむきに、期待と切望をもって

It's right after tryouts and it's a huge, huge deal that I have not tried out. ❶It is the talk of the school. It is ❷notorious. I go to Miss Hopkins.

No.

5   No—She comes to me.

She comes to me. She puts one of her ❸handsome hands, for I have looked at her hands and they are handsome, ❹square and firm and very, very clean with short, round nails. ❺Her watch is facedown on her wrist, not faceup like the other women's watches
10 and the band is dark brown leather, not thin and gold-looking like a bracelet. She puts her handsome, ❻competent hand on my shoulder. I feel it on me. It feels firm as if it ❼steadies me, but also light, like pulling me, like lifting me toward—toward—

I can smell her skin, like ❽Irish Spring soap, right next to me. I
15 ❾feel so much, like everything. And I can hear, I think, the sound of the air, its breath, as if the air is alive, around her ❿marvelous,

❶ It is the talk of the school: 学校じゅうその話で持ちきりだ

❷ notorious: 醜聞の、悪い評判が立った

❸ handsome: 形のいい。日本語ではもっぱら男性の容姿に用いるが、女性の威厳ある美しさにも使われるし、ここのように顔以外の姿・形についても言う。
　この文は She puts one of her handsome hands で始まり、おそらくは先生がその手をどこへ置いたかを言おうとしているが、手の美しさにいわば目を奪われて、言わないまま終わっている。

❹ square and firm: 角張ってしっかりしている

❺ Her watch is facedown on her wrist: 文字盤を見たときに手のひらが見えるような着け方。日本ではこれが女性の標準的な腕時計の着け方だが、ここでは逆。

❻ competent: 有能な

これは採用テストのすぐあとのこと。そしてテストを受けなかったというのはすごく、すごく大きなことだ。学校中の噂。とんでもない話。私はミス・ホプキンズのところに行く。

違う。

違う——ミス・ホプキンズが私のところに来るのだ。

彼女は私のところに来る。彼女はその形のいい片手を——私は彼女の手を前から見ているからそれが形よく角張っていてしっかりしていてすごくすごく綺麗で爪は短く丸いことを知っている、腕時計は女物の時計みたいに外側をじゃなく内側を向いていてバンドは焦げ茶の革でブレスレットのように細い金みたいな感じじゃないことを知っている——その形のいい、きびきびした片手を彼女は私の肩に置く。私はその手を肩に感じる。手は私を支えてくれるみたいにしっかり頼もしく感じられるけれど、同時に軽くも感じられる、私を引っぱってくれるみたいに、持ち上げてくれるみたいに——何に向けてだろう、何に……

彼女の肌の匂いが、アイリッシュ・スプリング石鹸みたいな匂いがすぐそばに感じられる。私はすごくいろんなことを、何もかもを感じる。そして私には聞こえる気がする、空気の音が、空気の息づく音が、まるで空気が彼女

---

❼ steadies <steady: 〜を安定させる

❽ Irish Spring soap: 実用的なデオドラント石鹸のブランド。

❾ feel so much, like everything: so much を like everything と言い換えてさらに強め、あえてつたない、うまく言葉が出てこないような感じにしている。

❿ marvelous: 素晴らしい

marvelous hands.

    She ❶leans her face down close to me and says, her breath like mint, "I heard you didn't try out for cheerleader."

    I cannot say—I don't—but I don't need to, no, not anything—

5   Because she knows.

    I look at her and, ❷for the first time ever, see behind her glasses. Her eyes are blue, lighter than blue eyes usually are, like ice, but also with a warmth to them, like ❸water you could fall into and it would sweep you away. I see her start to smile, her thin lips

10 somehow fuller, softening, and the skin ❹creasing around her mouth and I see the shine on her white, white teeth, one ❺canine slightly sharper than the rest. Her tongue is wet. I hear her ❻do this little laugh, then something else from inside her throat as she ❼removes, first, her plain black-framed glasses, then mine.

15   She tips my head back a bit and I close my eyes and tip my head further back and I am very still then feel something near my

---

❶ lean(s): 〜を傾ける

❷ for the first time ever: ever がなくても「初めて」だが、あることで意味がいっそう強まる。

❸ water you could fall into: そこに落ちてしまえる水、落ちてもいいなと思える水

❹ creasing <crease: 皺が寄る

❺ (a) canine: 犬歯

❻ do this little laugh: 小さな笑い声を立てる。do this ... という言い方は非常に口語的だが、それがくだけた感じというよりは、実感のこもった強い印象を残す。this は「a または the の一種の強調形；すでに特定化されているかのようにして提示することで聞き手に現実感・親近感を与える」(『リーダーズ英和辞典』)。

❼ remove(s): 〜を外す

の素敵な、すごく素敵な手の周りで生きているみたいに。

　彼女はかがみ込んで私に顔を近づけて言う、彼女の息がミントみたいに感じられる、「チアリーダーのテスト、受けなかったんだってね」

　私は何も言えない——言わない——でも言う必要はないのだ、何も、何も言わなくていいのだ——

　なぜなら彼女はわかってくれているから。

　私は彼女の顔を見て、そのとき初めて、彼女の眼鏡の奥が見える。彼女の目は青くて、普通の青い目より淡くて氷みたいだけど水みたいな暖かみもあってそこに飛び込んでさらわれてしまってもいい気がする。彼女の顔に笑みが浮かんでくるのが見える、薄い唇がいつもより何となくふっくらと和らいでいって、口の周りの皮膚にしわが寄ってその白い、真っ白い歯の輝きが見えてくる、一本の糸切り歯がほかよりほんの少し尖っている。舌が濡れている。彼女が小さな笑い声を上げるのが聞こえる、それから彼女の喉の奥から何か別の音がするのが聞こえて彼女はまず自分の地味な黒フレームの眼鏡を外しそれから私の眼鏡を外す。

　彼女は私の首を少しうしろに倒して私は目を閉じてもっと首を倒してそれからじっとしていると何かが肌のそばに感じられそしてささやく声が聞こえ

skin and hear a whisper, telling me—

I can't hear what she says.

Of course that didn't happen.

Not that, exactly. Not exactly then.

5   Her name was not Miss Hopkins. I was not thirteen.

But ❶someone sometime somethinged me. ❷There was some thing I almost felt, if not beside my body, then above me, in the air. Something or someone passed nearby. Or someone came toward me and I heard, almost, if not a voice, then something, then I saw

10 and someone kissed me.

Though neither that, exactly.

I kissed *her*.

It happened later.

15   She turned around a corner in the hall I couldn't see. (Though I have seen it since, yes, many times in memory and still I do.) She

❶ someone sometime somethinged me: somethinged はもちろん破格だが、「何かした」の意味であることは文脈から明白。

❷ There was some thing I almost felt, if not beside my body, then above me, in the air: ここで p. 70, ll. 11-12 の "... until I could almost feel against my skin, or at least in the air above my skin, a touch" という一節が読者の記憶によみがえり、出だしとクライマックスとが一気につながる。

る、私に何か言っているのが聞こえる……

　彼女が何と言っているのか私には聞こえない。

　もちろんそんなことは起こらなかった。

　文字どおりそういうふうには。文字どおりそのときには。

　彼女の名前はミス・ホプキンズじゃなかった。私は十三歳じゃなかった。

　でも誰かが、いつか、私に何かをしたのだ。何かあるのを私はほとんど感じたのだ、私の体のすぐそばではないとしても私の上の方に、空気のなかに。何かが、誰かが、そばを通っていった。それとも、誰かが私の方にやって来て私は聞いた、ほとんど聞いたのだ、声でないにしても何かを、それから目を上げると誰かが私にキスしたのだ。

　文字どおりには、それとも違う。

　私が彼女にキスしたのだ。

　それが起きたのはもっとあとのこと。

　彼女は私からは見えない廊下の角を曲がっていった（あとになってから私はそれを見たけれど、そう、記憶のなかで何度も見たし今も見ているけれど）。私が立っている廊下の窓ぎわの階段を彼女は降りていった。私はほ

stepped down ❶ the steps by the window in the hall I was standing in. I was talking to someone else who I forgot immediately ❷because already it had happened.

I saw, in the light of the late afternoon, the perfect light ❸*go over her.*
5 ❹*I saw illuminated her perfect face, her slightly open mouth. A brilliant light surrounded her. It* ❺*pulsed around her everywhere and I was almost blinded.* ❻*Her hair was black, her eyes were blue, her mouth was slightly open. There was a way she breathed, the way her chest and shoulders rose and fell. There was the way her throat moved when she* ❼*swallowed. There*
10 *was the line of the throat. There was* ❽*the cup in the flesh at the base of her throat. There was the light in the air around her. She was beautiful.*

I wanted to put my mouth on her. I wanted to eat her alive. I wanted ❾to possess her, to devour, to consume her. ❿I wanted to . . . something . . . her into next year and back and back again. I
15 wanted to, with her, ⓫annihilate myself.

I was, however, half her age.

For this and other reasons this did not occur.

---

❶ the steps by the window in the hall I was standing in: 私が立っていた廊下の窓際にあった階段

❷ because already it had happened: 普通なら because it had already happened だが、語順を普通と変えることでインパクトが強まる。

❸ go over her: 彼女の上を越えていく、彼女を覆っていく

❹ I saw illuminated her perfect face: これも普通なら I saw her perfect face illuminated。前後に何度も出てくる light という語と相まって、輝かしさ、神々しさが際立つ。

❺ pulse(d): 脈打つ

❻ Her hair was black, her eyes were blue ...: このあたりのセンテンスは、Her háir was bláck, her éyes are blúe ... というふうに、英語でもっとも正統的に美しいとされている iambic（弱強弱強……）のリズムになっている。レ

かの誰かと話していた、けれどそれが誰だったか私はたちまち忘れてしまった、なぜならすでにそれが起きたのだから。

　私は見た、夕方近くの光のなかで、完璧な光が彼女を覆うのを。彼女の完璧な顔が、わずかに開いた口が照らし出されるのを私は見た。まばゆい光が彼女を囲んでいた。彼女の周りいたるところで光は息づき、私はほとんど目がくらみそうだった。彼女の髪は黒く、目は青く、口はわずかに開いている。あの息づかい、胸と肩が上下するあの揺れ。唾を呑むときのあの喉の動き。あの喉の線。喉の下の方の、お椀のような凹み。周りの空気の光。彼女は綺麗だった。

　私は口で彼女に触れたかった。彼女を生きたまま食べてしまいたかった。彼女をわがものにし、貪り、食べ尽くしたかった。私はしたかった……何かを……彼女に……来年までずうっとしてまた何度も何度も戻ってきたかった。私はしたかった、彼女と一緒に自分をなくしてしまいたかった。

　けれど私は、彼女の半分の歳だった。

　そのせいで、ほかのいろんなことのせいで、これは起こらなかった。

　ベッカ・ブラウンの文章はこうしたリズムに関し非常に意識的である。

❼ swallow(ed): 喉をごくりとさせる、唾を呑む

❽ the cup in the flesh: 肌の凹み

❾ to possess her, to devour, to consume her: 彼女を所有し、貪り、食べ尽くす。だんだん「所有度」が強くなっていく。

❿ I wanted to ... something ...: ここは内容が過激すぎて書けないというよりは、自分でも何を求めているのか言葉にできない思いが胸の内で渦巻いていると考えるべきか。

⓫ annihilate: 〜を抹殺する

Not then.

Later.

Later I went back to her and took us to the bed. ❶Therein did we
5 do ❷what we were meant.

I still believe, ❸despite the rest, that this was good.

I loved her.

I saw in her ❹the possible. I saw ❺the real embodiment of what,
in some way, I had longed for years. ❻I saw she whom, though I
10 could not possess, I might hold for a time.

I believe what I remember.

I believe that what I saw and did continues in a place outside of
time, that it remains.

15 I believe that what remains occurs and will again.

I believe the vision I was shown, the body I was given.

I believe what I desired ❼was made manifest as love.

This is ❽what I tell of my religion.

---

❶ Therein: そこにおいて。古風な言葉が、儀式のような雰囲気を醸し出す。

❷ what we were meant: 普通なら what we were meant to do（私たちがす
る定めであること）だろうが、meant で切ることでインパクトが増す。

❸ despite the rest ... this was good: ほか（the rest）は good ではなかった
かもしれないが、という含み。

❹ the possible: ありうるもの、ありうべきもの

❺ the real embodiment of ...: 〜が真に形を成して現われたもの。embodi-
ment は抽象的に言えば「具現化」「体現」。

❻ I saw she whom: she は普通なら someone だろうが、古い英語では he や

そのときには。

あとになって。

あとになって私は彼女のもとに戻っていって彼女を連れて二人でベッドに入った。そこで私たちは定められていたことを為した。

ほかにはいろいろあったけれど、これは善いことだったといまも私は思う。

私は彼女を愛していた。

私は彼女のなかに、ありうべきものを見た。何年も前から心のどこかで憧れていたものが現実になった姿、肉体を帯びた姿を私は見た。わがものにはできなくてもつかのま抱きしめていられる人を私は見た。

自分が覚えていることを私は信じる。

自分が見たこと、したことが時を超えた場で続いていると、それがいまもあると私は信じる。

いまもあることは起きるのだと、これからもまた起きるのだと私は信じる。

自分に訪れた幻視を、自分に与えられた肉体を私は信じる。

自分が欲したことが愛として形を与えられたと私は信じる。

これが、私の宗教の話。

she をこのように関係代名詞で受ける用法もあった。

❼ was made manifest: 明白にされた＝はっきり形を与えられた

❽ what I tell of my religion: 私が私の宗教について語ること。tell about の方が普通だが、of の方が厳かな響きがある。

●

ちなみに

　この短篇が収められたレベッカ・ブラウンの作品集 *The End of Youth* (2003) には、"Nancy Booth, Wherever You Are" と題した、レズビアンとしての目覚めを描いた秀作がもう一本収められている。対照的なタイトルのつけ方からも窺えるとおり、"A Vision" が観念的・宗教的な次元に向かおうとしているのに対し、こちらはより現実的・具体的な出来事と思いが綴られている。

Linh Dinh

"!"

リン・ディン

難易度 1
★ ☆ ☆

リン・ディン
(Linh Dinh, 1963-　)

　サイゴン（現ホーチミン）に生まれ、11 歳で家族とともにアメリカへ渡る。本作「"!"」を収めた短篇集 *Blood and Soap* (2004) をはじめ、アメリカとベトナム両方を辛辣に諷刺した小説・詩多数。近年のノンフィクション *Postcards from the End of America* (2017) では痛烈なアメリカ現状批判を展開。

In **❶** *The Workers* newspaper of October 10, 2000, there was **❷** a curious item about a fake doctor. **❸** A certain Ngo Thi Nghe had been **❹** practicing medicine for over ten years on **❺** a false degree, which she **❻** procured, **❼** it is speculated, by killing its original

5 owner. She had all the **❽** accoutrements of medicine, a white suit, **❾** a thermometer, **❿** a bedpan, **⓫** a syringe, many bottles of pills, but no **⓬** formal knowledge of medicine. **⓭** In fact, she **⓮** had never gotten out of the eighth grade. **⓯** The mortality rate of her patients, however, was no higher than usual, and she was even defended by

10 some of her **⓰** clients, **⓱** after all the facts had come out, for saving their lives. "A most **⓲** compassionate doctor," said one elderly gentleman.

There are so many **⓳** scams nowadays that this case drew no special attention. Every day there are news reports of fake

15 lawyers, fake **⓴** architects, fake professors, and fake politicians doing business without the proper license or training. A most

---

❶ *The Workers* newspaper: この時点ではまだどこの国の話かわからないが、次行以降、ベトナム系とおぼしき名前がいくつも出てくる。そしてベトナムには事実、Người Lao Động (Workers) という名の新聞が存在する。

❷ a curious item: 奇妙な記事

❸ A certain ...: 〜とかいう人、〜なる人物

❹ practicing medicine <practice medicine: 医療に携わる

❺ a false degree: 虚偽の学位

❻ procure(d): 〜を手に入れる

❼ it is speculated: 〜と推測されている

❽ accoutrements: (その職業につきものの) 道具

❾ a thermometer: 体温計

❿ a bedpan: おまる

⓫ a syringe: 注射器

⓬ formal knowledge: 正規の知識

　2000 年 10 月 10 日付の『労働者』紙に、偽医者をめぐる奇妙な記事が載っていた。ゴー・ティ・ゲーという女性が 10 年以上にもわたって、虚偽の学位を使って医療に携わってきたというのである。彼女はこの学位を、本来の所有者を殺して入手したとされている。医者の道具は一通り、白衣、体温計、おまる、注射器、多数の薬瓶、等々揃っていたが、正規の医学知識はまったく持ち合わせていなかった。そもそも中学校すら出ていなかった。けれども、彼女の患者の死亡率は普通と較べて特に高いということはなく、事実がすべて明るみに出たあとも、何人かの患者が「命の恩人だ」と弁護さえしたのである。「あんなに優しい先生はいません」と、ある老紳士は言った。

　詐欺が横行している今日、この事件も取り立てて話題にはならなかった。ニュースを見れば毎日、偽弁護士、偽建築士、偽大学教授、偽政治家がしかるべき免許もなく訓練も受けずに仕事をしていたといった報道がなされてい

⑬ In fact: 事実、それどころか
⑭ had never gotten out of the eighth grade: the eighth grade は文字どおりには「第 8 学年」だが、たとえばアメリカだと 8 年制の小中学校も多いので、「第 8 学年を出ていない」は「中学校を終えていない」に等しい。
⑮ The mortality rate: 死亡率
⑯ client(s): 依頼人、顧客。ここでは patients のこと。
⑰ after all the facts had come out: すべての事実が出てきたあとで＝事実がすべて明るみに出ても
⑱ compassionate: 思いやりある
⑲ scam(s): 詐欺、ぺてん
⑳ architect(s): 建築家

curious case in recent memory, however, is that of Ho Muoi, who ❶was accused of being a fake English teacher. From ❷perusing ❸innumerable newspaper ❹accounts, I was able to ❺piece together ❻the following:

5   Ho Muoi was born in 1952 in Ky Dong Village. His family made ❼firecrackers until they were ❽banned because of the war. ❾Thereafter the father became an alcoholic and left the family. Although Ho Muoi was only six at the time, he ❿knew enough to ⓫swear that he would never mention or even think of his father's
10 name again. His mother supported the children, all five of them, by carrying water and ⓬night soil ⓭for hire, a ⓮backbreaking labor that made her shorter by several inches. She also made ⓯meat dumplings that she sold on ⓰special occasions.

    Ky Dong Village is known for a festival, held every January
15 5th, ⓱in honor of ⓲a legendary general of a ⓳mythical king who fought against a real enemy two or three thousand years ago. The festival ⓴features a duck-catching demonstration, a wrestling

---

❶ was accused of: 〜のかどで起訴された
❷ perusing <peruse: 〜を熟読する
❸ innumerable: 無数の
❹ account(s): 記述
❺ piece together: （話などを）まとめる
❻ the following: 以下の話
❼ firecracker(s): 爆竹
❽ ban(ned): 〜を禁止する
❾ Thereafter: それ以来
❿ knew enough to ...: 〜するだけの知恵があった
⓫ swear: 〜を誓う
⓬ night soil: 屎尿

る。だが近年記憶に残っているきわめて奇異な例といえば、偽英語教師として告発されたホー・ムオイであろう。もろもろの新聞の記述を仔細に検討した結果、私は以下のような物語を組み立てるに至った。

　ホー・ムオイは1952年、キー・ドン村に生まれた。家は爆竹を作っていたが、やがて戦争で禁止された。その後父親は酒浸りになって家を出ていった。当時ホー・ムオイはまだ6歳であったが、父親の名を二度と口にしまい、考えもしまいと誓うだけの知恵はすでについていた。母親は子供5人を育てるために、水と糞尿の運搬を請け負い、その重労働で背が10センチ以上縮んだ。加えて、肉団子を作って祭日などに売った。

　キー・ドン村は、毎年1月5日に催される、2000年だか3000年だか昔に神話の王に仕えた伝説の将軍が本物の敵と戦ったのをたたえる祭で知られる。祭の呼び物は、鴨獲り芸、少年格闘技大会、少女肉団子作りコンテスト、

⓭ for hire: 雇われて、請け負って
⓮ backbreaking:（背中を痛めそうなほど）ひどく骨の折れる
⓯ meat dumpling(s): 肉団子
⓰ special occasion(s): 特別な行事
⓱ in honor of ...: 〜を祝って
⓲ a legendary general: 伝説の将軍
⓳ mythical: 神話の
⓴ feature(s): 〜を呼び物とする

❶tournament for the boys, a meat dumpling making contest for the girls, and, until it was banned because of the war, a ❷procession of firecrackers.

Those who've ❸witnessed this procession of firecrackers ❹describe a scene where boys and girls and ❺gay men ❻jiggle ❼papier-mâché animals and ❽genitals ❾strung from bamboo sticks ❿amid the smoke and ⓫din of a million firecrackers.

But the excitement from the festival only came once a year. For the rest of the time, the villagers ⓬were preoccupied with ⓭the tedium and anxieties of daily life. Most of the young men ⓮were drafted into the army, sent away and never came back, but the war never came directly to Ky Dong Village.

When Ho Muoi was ten, his mother ⓯enrolled him in school for the first time. He was ⓰slow and it took him a year to learn the alphabet. He could never ⓱figure out how to ⓲add or subtract. His worst ⓳subject, however, was ⓴geography. It was ㉑inconceivable to him that there are hundreds of countries in the world, each

---

❶ (a) tournament: 勝ち抜き試合

❷ (a) procession: 行列、行進

❸ witness: 〜を目撃する、見る

❹ describe: 〜を記述する、説明する

❺ gay: 陽気な

❻ jiggle: 〜を揺さぶる

❼ papier-mâché: 張り子の（発音は /pèɪpərməʃéɪ/ など）

❽ genital(s): 生殖器

❾ strung <string: 〜を紐でくくる

❿ amid: 〜の只中で

⓫ din: 騒音

⓬ were preoccupied with ...: 〜で頭が一杯だった

そして戦争で禁止されるまでは爆竹行進であった。

この爆竹行進を見た人々が語るところによれば、無数の爆竹の煙と轟音のなか、少年少女と陽気な男たちが竹の棒につないだ張り子の動物やら生殖器やらを揺さぶりながら練り歩くのだという。

けれども、祭の熱狂は年に一度訪れるにすぎない。残りの日々、村人たちの頭の中は日々の暮らしの退屈と不安で一杯であった。若者の大半は徴兵されてよそに送られ、二度と戻ってこなかったが、戦争が直接キー・ドン村に来ることはついぞなかった。

ホー・ムオイが10歳になると、母親は彼を学校に通わせた。呑み込みはすこぶる悪く、アルファベットを学ぶのに一年かかった。足し算や引き算はどうしても覚えられなかった。だが一番の苦手は地理だった。世界には何百もの国があって、それぞれ違う話し言葉を持っているという事態が、彼には

⓭ the tedium and anxieties: 退屈とさまざまな不安
⓮ were drafted: 徴兵された
⓯ enroll(ed): ～を入学させる
⓰ slow: (もの覚え・理解などが) 遅い
⓱ figure out ...: ～を理解する、わかる
⓲ add or subtract: 足し算や引き算をする
⓳ (a) subject: 科目
⓴ geography: 地理
㉑ inconceivable: 想像も及ばない

with a different **❶**spoken language. **❷**Every single word of his own
language felt so **❸**inevitable that he thought it would be a crime
against nature to call a cow or a bird anything different.

Ho Muoi could not even **❹**conceive of *two* countries sharing
5 this same earth. "Countries" in **❺**the plural sounds like either **❻**a
tautology or **❼**an oxymoron. "Country," "earth," and "universe"
were all **❽**synonymous in his mind.

Ho Muoi's teacher was a very **❾**sophisticated young man from
Hanoi. He was the only one within a fifty-mile **❿**radius who had
10 ever read a newspaper or who owned even a single book. He
even **⓫**fancied himself a poet in his **⓬**spare time. He **⓭**did not mind
teaching **⓮**a bunch of village **⓯**idiots, however, because it **⓰**spared
him from the bombs and **⓱**landmines that were the fate of his
⓲contemporaries. In the evening he **⓳**could be found in his dark
15 room reading a Russian novel. The teacher was short and **⓴**scrawny
and had a habit of shutting his eyes tight and **㉑**sticking his lips out

---

❶ (a) spoken language: 話し言葉
❷ Every single word: every word 以上に「どの一語も」という感じが強調される。
❸ inevitable: 必然的な、それ以外ありえない
❹ conceive of ...: 〜を想像する
❺ the plural: 複数形（⇔ the singular）
❻ a tautology: 類語反復。「馬から落ちて落馬する」"In my opinion, I think ..."
など。
❼ an oxymoron: 矛盾語法。"an honest politician" など。
❽ synonymous: 同義の
❾ sophisticated: 知的に洗練された
❿ radius: 半径

想像もつかなかった。自分自身の言語の単語一つひとつがまったくの必然に感じられたので、牛なり鳥なりを違う名で呼ぶなんて自然に対する犯罪としか思えなかった。

そもそもホー・ムオイは、二つの国が地球を共有しているという事態さえ思い描けなかった。「国々」と複数で言うのは同じことのくり返しか言葉の矛盾かに思えた。「国」「地球」「宇宙」、彼の頭の中ではみな同義語だった。

ホー・ムオイの教師は、ハノイから来た非常に洗練された青年であった。半径50マイルの範囲で、新聞を読んだことがあるのは、そもそも一冊でも本を所有しているのは、この男以外にいなかった。空いた時間には独り、詩人を気どったりもした。それでも、村の阿呆どもを教えるのは嫌ではなかった。そのおかげで同世代の連中の運命たる爆弾と地雷から逃れられるのだから。晩になると、彼が薄暗い部屋でロシアの小説を読んでいる姿が見受けられた。教師は小男で痩せていて、集中すると目をぎゅっと閉じて唇をつき出

⓫ fancied himself a poet: 自分は詩人だぞと思っていた、詩人気取りでいた
⓬ spare time: 空いた時間
⓭ did not mind teaching ...: ～を教えることを嫌がらなかった
⓮ a bunch of: 沢山の。「有象無象」「十把一からげ」といった含みを伴うことが多い。
⓯ idiot(s): 阿呆
⓰ spare(d): （苦労・苦痛を）免れさせる
⓱ landmine(s): 地雷
⓲ contemporaries: 同年輩の人々
⓳ could be found ... ing: ～している姿が見られた
⓴ scrawny: 痩せこけた
㉑ stick(ing) ... out: ～を突き出す

when **❶**concentrating. Still, it was **❷**odd that he **❸**managed to attract
no women in a village almost entirely **❹**emptied of its young men.

❺Whenever this teacher **❻**was exasperated with his **❼**charge he
would shout "!" but no one knew what the word meant or **❽**what
language it was in so it **❾**was dismissed as a sort of **❿**a sneeze or a
clearing of the throat.

At twelve, something happened to Ho Muoi that would change
⓫his whole outlook on life. He was walking home from school
when he saw a crowd gathering around three men who were at
least **⓬**two heads taller than the average person. The men had a
pink, almost red **⓭**complexion and their hair **⓮**varied from a bright
orange to a **⓯**whitish yellow. They were **⓰**not unfriendly and
⓱allowed people to **⓲**tug at the abundant hair growing on their
arms. "Wonderful creatures," Ho Muoi thought as he stared at
them, **⓳**transfixed. One of the men noticed Ho Muoi and started to
say something. The words **⓴**were rapid, like curses, but the man
㉑was smiling as he was saying them. All eyes turned to look at

❶ concentrating <concentrate: 集中する
❷ odd: 妙な
❸ managed to attract no women: 一人の女の気も惹かなかった。manage to は can に近いが、「なかなかできることではない」というニュアンスを伴うことが多い。
❹ emptied of ...: ～がなくなっている
❺ Whenever: ～するたびに
❻ was exasperated: 苛立った
❼ charge: 受け持った人々（特に子供）
❽ what language it was in: それが何語の（中の）言葉なのか
❾ was dismissed as ...: ～として片付けられた
❿ a sneeze: くしゃみ

す癖があった。それでも、若い男が皆無に近い村にあって、彼が一人の女の気も惹かずにいるのは、妙といえば妙であった。

生徒たちに苛（いら）つくたび、この教師は「！」と叫んだが、その言葉がどういう意味なのか、そもそも何語の言葉なのか、誰にもわからなかったので、一種のくしゃみ、咳払いのようなものとして片付けられた。

12歳のとき、ホー・ムオイの人生観を根本から変える出来事が起きた。学校からの帰り道、3人の男の周りに人だかりが出来ているところにホー・ムオイは出くわした。男たちは並の人間より少なくとも頭2つ分背が高かった。ピンク色の、ほとんど赤色の肌をしていて、髪は明るいオレンジから白っぽい黄色まで幅があった。3人ともそれなりに友好的で、腕にふさふさ生えた毛を人々が引っぱってもべつに文句を言わない。「何て素晴らしい生き物だろう」とホー・ムオイは彼らに見とれながら思った。と、男たちの一人がホー・ムオイに目をとめ、何か言い出した。それは早口の呪いみたいに聞こえたが、言いながら男はニコニコ笑っていた。すべての目がホー・ムオイに

---

❶ his whole outlook on life: 彼の人生観全体

❷ two heads taller: 頭二つ分背が高い

❸ complexion: 肌の（特に顔の）色

❹ varied from ... to ...: 〜から〜まで、それぞれ違っていた

❺ whitish: 白っぽい

❻ not unfriendly: 進んで友好的とまでは行かないが、さりとて愛想が悪くはない、という感じ。

❼ allowed people to ...: 人々が〜しても文句は言わなかった、という感じ。

❽ tug: 引っぱる

❾ transfixed: 釘付けになって

❿ were rapid, like curses: 呪いの言葉のように早口だった

㉑ was smiling as he was saying them: 言いながらニコニコ笑っていた

Ho Muoi. Some people started to laugh and he wanted to ❶laugh along with them but he could not. Suddenly his face ❷flushed and he felt ❸ an intense hatred against these foreign men. If he had a gun he would have shot them ❹already. Without ❺premeditation
5 he ❻blurted out "!" then ran away.

When Ho Muoi got home his heart was still beating wildly. The excitement of blurting out ❼a magical word, ❽a word he did not know the meaning of, ❾was overwhelming. He also remembered the look of shock on the man's face after the word had left his
10 mouth. He repeated "!" several times and felt its power each time.

Ho Muoi would think about this ❿incident for years afterward. He recalled how he ⓫was initially enraged by ⓬a series of foreign words, and that he had ⓭retaliated with a foreign word of his own. In his mind, foreign words ⓮became equated with a terrible power.
15 The fact that his own language would be foreign to a foreigner ⓯never occurred to him.

The incident also ⓰turned Ho Muoi into a celebrity. The villagers would ⓱recall with relish ⓲how one of their own, a

---

❶ laugh along with them: 一緒に笑う。along は人に合わせて一緒にやる感じが加わる。

❷ flush(ed): (顔が) 赤らむ

❸ an intense hatred against ...: 〜への激しい憎悪

❹ already: 今すぐ、さっさと

❺ premeditation: 前もって考えること

❻ blurt(ed) out ...: 〜と口走る、思わず〜と言う

❼ a magical word: 魔法の言葉

❽ a word he did not know the meaning of: 自分でも意味を知らない単語

❾ was overwhelming: 圧倒的だった

❿ (an) incident: 出来事

注がれた。何人かはハハハと笑い出し、ホー・ムオイも一緒に笑いたかったが、できなかった。突然顔が火照ってきて、これら外国人に対する激しい憎しみが湧いてきた。もし銃を持っていたら、さっさと3人とも撃ち殺してしまったことだろう。何も考えずに彼は「！」と叫び、走り去った。

　家にたどり着いても、心臓はまだドキドキ鳴っていた。魔法の言葉、意味も知らぬ言葉を口にした興奮は圧倒的であった。言葉が彼の口を離れたあとに男の顔に浮かんだショックの表情も思い出された。「！」と何度かくり返しホー・ムオイは言い、言うたびにその力を感じた。

　その後何年も、ホー・ムオイはこの一件についてくり返し思いをめぐらすことになる。あのとき自分が、まず外国の言葉の連なりを聞いて憤り、次に自ら外国語を発して反撃したことを思い起こした。彼の頭のなかで、外国語というものは恐ろしい力と結びついていった。彼自身の言語も外国人にとっては外国語なのだという事実にはいっこうに思い至らなかった。

　事件はまた、ホー・ムオイを有名人にした。村人たちは、自分たちの一員の、12歳の少年が、外国人を相手にして、相手の言葉で呪いを投げつけ「対

⓫ was initially enraged: 最初は激怒していた

⓬ a series of ...: ひと連なりの〜

⓭ retaliate(d): 報復する

⓮ became equated with ...: 〜と等価になった

⓯ never occurred to him: まったく思いあたらなかった

⓰ turned Ho Muoi into a celebrity: ホー・ムオイを有名人にした

⓱ recall with relish: 思い出しては悦に入る

⓲ how one of their own ...: こういう場合の how は「どのように〜」と訳すよりは、「〜したときの様子」「〜したこと」くらいに訳した方がしっくり来ることが多い。one of their own: 自分たちの一人

twelve-year-old boy, had "❶stood up to a foreigner" by ❷hurling a curse at him in his own language. Many ❸marveled at the boy's ❹intelligence for knowing how to use a foreign word, heard maybe once or twice ❺in passing, ❻on just the right occasion and ❼with 5 authority. They even ❽suggested to the schoolteacher ❾that he teach "the boy genius" all the foreign words from his Russian novels.

The schoolteacher never ❿got around to doing this. He was drafted soon after, sent south, and ⓫was never heard from again. As for Ho Muoi, he ⓬became convinced that, ⓭given the opportuni-10 ty, he could quickly learn any foreign language. This opportunity came after Ho Muoi himself was drafted into the army.

His ⓮battalion ⓯served in the Central Highlands, along the Truong Son Mountain, guarding ⓰supply lines. They ⓱rarely made contact with the enemy but whenever they did, Ho Muoi ⓲acquitted 15 himself ⓳miserably. He often froze and had to be ⓴literally ㉑kicked into action. What was ㉒perceived by his ㉓comrades as ㉔cowardice,

---

❶ stood up to <stand up to ...: 〜に勇敢に立ち向かう
❷ hurl(ing): 〜を浴びせる
❸ marvel(ed) at ...: 〜に驚く
❹ intelligence: 聡明さ
❺ in passing: ついでに
❻ on just the right occasion: まさにぴったりの機会に
❼ with authority: 威厳をもって、堂々と
❽ suggest(ed): (〜してはどうかと) 提案する
❾ that he teach "the boy genius" ...: "he teach" は誤記ではない。suggest, demand など「提唱、要求」を表わす動詞のあとに that 節が来ると、その中の動詞は原形（厳密には「仮定法現在」）になる。
❿ got around to <get around to ...: 〜する機会にたどり着く
⓫ was never heard from: 二度と連絡がなかった。hear from ...: 〜から連絡を受ける

等に渡りあった」ことを鼻高々思い起こした。せいぜい一、二度何かのついでに聞いただけの外国語を、絶好のタイミングで堂々と使える少年の賢さに多くの者が感心した。彼らは教師に、あんたの読んでるロシアの小説に出てくる外国の言葉を「神童」にそっくり教えたらどうかね、とさえ言った。

　教師はこれを実行するには至らなかった。その後まもなく徴兵されて、南に送られ、それっきり消息を絶ったのである。ホー・ムオイ本人は、機会さえあれば自分はどんな外国語でもたちどころに習得できるのだと確信するに至った。そしてその機会は、ホー・ムオイ自身が軍隊に徴兵されてしばらくしてから訪れた。

　彼の歩兵大隊は、中央高地のチュオン・ソン山沿いに配置され、兵站線を護る任を担った。敵とはめったに遭遇しなかったが、たまに遭遇するたび、ホー・ムオイは何とも情けないふるまいしかできなかった。凍りついてしまうこともしばしばで、文字どおり蹴飛ばされないと動けもしなかった。しかし、仲間たちの目に臆病さと映ったものは、肉体的な痛みを怖がる気持ちと

❷ became convinced: 確信するようになった

❸ given the opportunity: 機会があれば

❹ (a) battalion: 大隊

❺ serve(ed): 軍務に就く

❻ supply lines: 補給線、兵站線

❼ rarely made contact: めったに接触しなかった

❽ acquitted himself <acquit oneself: (難しい場面で) ～にふるまう

❾ miserably: 無残に

⓴ literally: 文字どおり

㉑ kicked into action <kick ... into action: ～を蹴って行動させる

㉒ perceive(d): ～を認識する、受け取る

㉓ comrade(s): 仲間、戦友

㉔ cowardice: 臆病

however, was **❶**not so much a fear of physical pain as the **❷**dread that he **❸**would not be allowed to **❹**fulfill his destiny.

The war was **❺**an outrage, Ho Muoi thought, not because it was **❻**wiping out thousands of people a day, the young, the old, and the unborn, but that it could **❼**exterminate **❽**a man of destiny like himself. **❾**And yet he understood that wars also provide many lessons to those who survived them. A war is a working man's university. Knowing that, he almost **❿**felt grateful.

Ho Muoi also had **⓫**the superstition (or the inspiration) that if the war **⓬**eliminates a single book from this earth, then that would be a greater loss **⓭**than all the lives wasted. The death of a man **⓮**affects three or four other individuals, **⓯**at most. **⓰**Its significance is symbolic and sentimental, but the loss of a single book is **⓱**tangible, **⓲**a disaster which should be **⓳**mourned forever by all of mankind. The **⓴**worth of a society is measured by how many books

---

❶ not so much ... as ...: not so much A as B で「A というより B だ」。

❷ dread: 恐怖、不安

❸ would not be allowed to ...: 〜することを許されないだろう＝〜する機会もなく終わってしまうだろう

❹ fulfill his destiny: 運命を遂げる

❺ an outrage: 非道な行ない

❻ wiping out <wipe out ...: 〜を一掃する

❼ exterminate: 〜を根絶する

❽ a man of destiny: 大きな運命を担う人間

❾ And yet: とはいえ。この意味の yet は but とそんなに変わらないが、and と一緒にも使えるところが違う。

❿ felt grateful: ありがたく思った

⓫ the superstition (or the inspiration): 迷信（あるいは霊感）。inspiration も superstition と同様無根拠だが、それが単なる迷妄ではなく、一種神がかり的な着想だという含み。

いうよりも、むしろ、己が運命を全うせずに終わってしまうのではないかという恐れであった。

　戦争は非道だ、とホー・ムオイは思ったが、それは毎日老いも若きも生まれざる者も数千人が抹殺されているからではなく、自分のような大いなる運命を負った人間が消されてしまいかねないからである。とはいえ、戦争がまた、それを生き抜く者たちに多くを教えていることも彼は理解していた。戦争とは働く人間の大学である。そう実感すると、ほとんど感謝に近い念が湧いてきた。

　ホー・ムオイはまた、もし戦争が地上から書物を一冊でも消滅させてしまうなら、その喪失は無駄にされた生命すべてよりも大きいのだという迷信に（あるいは霊感に）囚われていた。一人の人間の死は、せいぜい3、4人の心に影響を及ぼすにすぎず、その意味は抽象的かつ感傷的なものでしかない。だが一冊の書物の消滅はもっと具体的であり、全人類によって永遠に悼まれるべき大惨事なのだ。ひとつの社会の値打ちは、その社会が生み出した本の

---

❷ eliminate(s): 〜を抹殺する

❸ than all the lives wasted: 無駄にされたすべての生命以上に

❹ affect(s): 〜に影響・変化を及ぼす

❺ at most: せいぜい、多くて

❻ Its significance is symbolic and sentimental: その意味は象徴的・感傷的である（にすぎない）

❼ tangible: 実質的な、手に取れるような（上の symbolic and sentimental と対比されている）

❽ a disaster: 大惨事

❾ mourn(ed): 〜を嘆き悲しむ

❿ worth: 価値

it has produced. ❶This, from a man who had never actually read a book. Ho Muoi had seen so few books, he ❷could not tell one from another; they were all equal in his mind. He ❸never suspected that war is ❹the chief generator of books. A war is a thinking man's
5 university.

In 1970 or 1971, after a brief ❺skirmish, they caught an American soldier whom they ❻kept for about thirty days. The ❼prisoner was made to ❽march along with Ho Muoi's battalion until he fell ill and died (he ❾was not badly injured). This man was given the
10 same ❿ration as the others but the food ⓫did not agree with him. Once, they even gave him an extra ⓬helping of ⓭orangutan meat, thinking it would ⓮restore his health.

As the prisoner ⓯sank into delirium,the color ⓰drained from his face but his eyes ⓱lit up. He would ⓲blather for hours ⓳on end. No
15 one paid him any attention ⓴but Ho Muoi. In his tiny notebook he would record ㉑as much of the man's ㉒rambling as possible. These

---

❶ This, from a man who ...: ～する人間がこんなことを言う（する）のだ。
  This from a ... の形でよく使われる。
❷ could not tell one from another: 見分けがつかなかった
❸ never suspected that ...: ～とは考えもしなかった
❹ the chief generator of ...: ～を生み出す主な要因
❺ (a) skirmish: 小ぜりあい
❻ kept <keep: ～を拘留する
❼ (a) prisoner: 捕虜
❽ march: 行進する
❾ was not badly injured: ひどい怪我をしていたわけではなかった
❿ ration: （配給の）食糧
⓫ did not agree with him: 体に合わなかった
⓬ (a) helping: （食べ物・料理の）一人前

数によって測られる。……といったことを、実際に本を読んだことは一度も
ない人間が考えたのである。本などろくに見たこともなかったから、さまざ
まな本を区別しようもなかった。彼の頭のなかですべての本は等価であった。
戦争こそ本を生み出す主たる要因ではないか、などとは考えもしなかった。
戦争とは考える人間の大学である。

　1970 年だか 71 年だかに、隊は短い小ぜりあいの末にアメリカ人兵士を一
人捕らえ、およそ 30 日捕虜にしていた。捕虜はホー・ムオイの大隊ととも
に行軍させられたが、やがて病気になって死んだ。怪我がひどかったのでは
ない。他人と同じ食糧を配給されたものの、それがこの男には合わなかった
のである。あるときなど、回復の足しになるかと、オランウータンの肉を二
人分与えてみたが、効き目はなかった。

　譫妄状態に陥っていくにつれて、捕虜の顔から血の気が引いていったが、
目はギラギラ光っていた。男は何時間もうわごとを言った。誰も彼に構わな
かったが、ホー・ムオイだけは別だった。小さなメモ帳に、彼は捕虜の言っ
た取りとめのない言葉をできる限り書き留めた。聞こえた音をそのまま書い

⓭ orangutan: オランウータン（発音は /əræŋətæn/ など）

⓮ restore: 〜を回復させる

⓯ sank into delirium: 譫妄状態に陥った

⓰ drain(ed):（血の気などが）引く

⓱ lit up <light up: 輝く

⓲ blather: べらべら喋る

⓳ on end: ぶっ続けで

⓴ but Ho Muoi: ホー・ムオイ以外は

㉑ as much ... as possible: 〜をできるだけ多く

㉒ rambling: 取りとめのない喋り

❶phonetic notations became the source for Ho Muoi's English lessons after the war. I've seen pages from the notebook. Its lines often ran ❷diagonally from one corner to another. A ❸typical ❹run-on sentence: ❺"hoo he hoo ah utta ma nut m pap m home."

5 The notebook also ❻includes ❼numerous sketches of the American. Each portrait ❽was meant as a visual clue to the words ❾swarming around it. Ho Muoi's skills as an artist were so poor, however, that ❿the face depicted always appeared the same, that ⓫of a young man, any man, really, who ⓬has lost all touch with the
10 world.

Ho Muoi was hoping his ⓭unit would catch at least one more American ⓮so he could continue his English lesson, but this ⓯tutor never ⓰materialized, unfortunately.

Though all the English he had ⓱was contained within a single
15 notebook, Ho Muoi ⓲was not discouraged. The American must have spoken ⓳just about every word there was in his native

---

❶ phonetic notation(s): 音を書きとめた記録

❷ diagonally: 斜めに

❸ typical: 典型的な

❹ (a) run-on sentence: ピリオドで終わるべきところにピリオドがなくだらだら続いているセンテンスのこと。

❺ "hoo he hoo ah utta ma nut m pap m home": 故郷に帰りたかったアメリカ兵のうわごとの中から、home だけは正しく聴きとれたということだろうか。そう考えると、"ma" と "pap" も両親のことかと思えてくる。

❻ include(s): 〜を含む

❼ numerous: たくさんの

❽ was meant as a visual clue: 視覚的な手がかりとして意図されていた＝視覚的なヒントのつもりで描かれていた

❾ swarm(ing) around: 周りに群がる

❿ the face depicted: 描かれた顔

たこの記録が、戦後にホー・ムオイが行なった英語の授業の土台となったのである。そのメモ帳の何ページかは私も見た。一方の隅から別の隅へと行が斜めに流れている箇所も多かった。ずらずら書き綴られたセンテンスの一例を挙げれば——「フー・ヒー・フー・アー・アタ・マ・ナト・ム・パプ・ム・ホーム」。

メモ帳にはアメリカ人兵士のスケッチもたくさん入っている。スケッチ一つひとつが、その顔の周りに群がっている言葉たちを説明する図解として意図されていた。だがホー・ムオイの画才は乏しく、描かれた顔はどれも同じに見えた。若い男の顔、べつに誰でもいい、とにかく、世界との接触をいっさい失ってしまった男の顔。

英語の勉強を続けられるよう、自分の部隊がせめてもう一人アメリカ人をつかまえないものかとホー・ムオイは期待していた。だがあいにく、第二の個人教師はいつまで経っても現われなかった。

手元にある英語はたった一冊のメモ帳に収まったものだけだったが、ホー・ムオイはめげなかった。あのアメリカ人はきっと、母国語にある単語をほぼすべて口にしたにちがいない、と彼は考えた。何しろ夜ごとあんなに夢中で

❶ of a young man, any man, really: 一人の若者の——いや、誰だっていい、一人の誰かの
❷ has lost all touch with the world: 世界との接触をすべて失った
❸ (a) unit: 部隊
❹ so he could continue his English lesson: 英語のレッスンを続けられるように
❺ (a) tutor: 個人教師
❻ materialize(d): 出現する
❼ was contained within ...: ～の中に収められていた
❽ was not discouraged: くじけなかった
❾ just about every word there was in his native language: 彼の母語の中にあるほぼ全単語

language, **❶**he reasoned, through all those nights of **❷**raving. And the **❸**invisible words **❹**can be inferred from the visible ones.

Words are like numbers, he**❺**further reasoned, **❻**a closed system with a small set of **❼**self-generated rules. And **❽**words arranged on a page **❾**resemble **❿**a dull, monotonous painting. If one could look at the **⓫**weirdest picture and **⓬**decipher, **⓭**sooner or later, **⓮**its organizing principle, **⓯**why can't one do the same with words?

Everything seems **⓰**chaotic at first, but nothing is chaotic. One can read anything: ants **⓱**crawling on the ground; **⓲**pimples on a face; trees in a forest. **⓳**Fools will argue with you about this, but any **⓴**surface can be deciphered. The entire world, **㉑**as seen from an airplane, is just a **㉒**warped surface.

A man **㉓**may fancy he's making **㉔**an abstract painting, but **㉕**there is no such thing as an abstract painting, only **㉖**abstracted ones. Every **㉗**horizontal surface is a landscape because it **㉘**features

---

❶ he reasoned: 〜と彼は推論した

❷ raving: うわごと

❸ invisible: 目に見えない

❹ can be inferred from ...: 〜から推論できる

❺ further: さらに

❻ a closed system: 閉じた系、自己完結したシステム

❼ self-generated rules: 自然発生した規則

❽ words arranged on a page: ページ上に並べられた単語

❾ resemble: 〜に似ている

❿ a dull, monotonous painting: 退屈で単調な絵画

⓫ weird(est): 変な

⓬ decipher: 〜を解読する

⓭ sooner or later: 遅かれ早かれ、いずれは

⓮ its organizing principle: その構成原理

喋りつづけたのだから。それに、見えない言葉は見える言葉から推論すればいい。

言葉は数のようなものだ、とホー・ムオイはさらに考えた。自然発生した一握りの規則を持つ閉じたシステムなのだ、と。紙の上に並べられた言葉は、地味で単調な絵画に似ている。どんなに風変わりな絵画だって、じっくり見てみればいずれその構成原理を解明できるのなら、言葉についても同じことができるはずでは？

何ごとも一目見ただけだと混沌として見えるが、混沌などというものは存在しない。その気になれば何だって解読できる。地面を這う蟻たち。顔に浮かんだニキビ。森のなかの木々。馬鹿は反論するだろうが、いかなる表層も判読可能なのだ。世界全体にしても、飛行機から見ればわかるように、歪んだ表面以上のものではない。

本人は抽象画を描いているつもりでも、抽象画などというものはありえない。抽象的に描かれた絵画があるだけだ。水平な面は水平線を含んでいるがゆえにつねに一個の風景である（したがって旅、自己からの逃避、届かない

---

❶⑤ why can't one ...?: 〜できてもいいではないか

❶⑥ chaotic: 混沌とした

❶⑦ crawl(ing): 這う

❶⑧ pimple(s): にきび

❶⑨ Fools will argue with you: 馬鹿は反論するだろう

❷⓪ (a) surface: 表面、表層

❷① as seen from an airplane: 飛行機から見れば

❷② warped: 歪んだ

❷③ may fancy:（自分では）〜と思うかもしれない

❷④ an abstract painting: 抽象画

❷⑤ there is no such thing as ...: 〜などというものは存在しない

❷⑥ abstracted: 抽象化された、抽象的に描かれた

❷⑦ horizontal: 水平な（⇔ vertical）

❷⑧ features a horizon: 水平線を（主要な要素として）提示している

a horizon (❶ thus ❷ implying a journey, escape from ❸ the self, and ❹ the unreachable). Every ❺ vertical surface is either a door or a portrait (thus implying a house, ❻ another being, yourself as another being, and the unreachable). And all colors have ❼ shared

5 and private associations. Red may ❽ inspire horror in one culture, ❾ elation in another, but ❿ it is still red, is still blood. Green always ⓫ evokes trees and a pretty green dress.

Ho Muoi also believed that anything made by man can be ⓬ duplicated: a chair, a gun, a language, ⓭ provided one has ⓮ the

10 raw materials, ⓯ as he did, with his one notebook of phonetic notations. If one can ⓰ break apart a clock and ⓱ reassemble it, one can ⓲ scramble up phonetic notations and ⓳ rearrange them in newer combinations, thus ⓴ ending up with not just a language, but a literature.

15 At the time of his ㉑ arrest, Ho Muoi was teaching hundreds of students ㉒ beginning, intermediate, and advanced English three

---

❶ thus: かくして
❷ imply(ing): 〜を示唆する
❸ the self: 自己
❹ the unreachable: 届かないもの
❺ vertical: 垂直の
❻ another being: 他人、他者
❼ shared and private associations: 多くの人が共有している連想と、個人に限られた連想
❽ inspire: （ある感情・霊感を）起こさせる
❾ elation: 高揚
❿ it is still red: それでも赤は赤だ
⓫ evoke(s): 〜を呼び起こす
⓬ duplicate(d): 〜を複製する

ものを示唆する）。垂直な面はすべて扉か肖像である（したがって家、他人、他人としての自分、届かないものを示唆する）。色にもすべて社会的・個人的連想が伴う。赤はある文化では恐怖を、またある文化では高揚を喚起するが、それでも赤はやはり赤であり血である。緑はつねに、木々と、綺麗な緑色のドレスを思い起こさせる。

　ホー・ムオイはさらに、人間が作ったものはすべて複製可能だと信じた。椅子、銃、言語。素材さえあれば何だって複製できる。そして自分にはもろもろの音を記録したメモ帳があるのだ。時計を分解して組み立て直すことができるなら、音の記録をいったんバラバラにして新しい組合せを作り出すことも可能なはずだ。こうして、一個の言語のみならず、一個の文学を作り上げることも夢ではない。

　逮捕された当時、ホー・ムオイは毎週三晩、何百人もの生徒を相手に、初級、中級、上級の英語クラスを教えていた。25年のあいだ、何百万という語彙

⓭ provided ...: 仮に〜とすれば

⓮ the raw materials: 原料

⓯ as he did: 彼が（素材を）持っていたように＝そして彼には素材があったわけだが

⓰ break apart ...: 〜を分解する

⓱ reassemble: 〜を組み立て直す

⓲ scramble up ...: 〜をごちゃ混ぜにする

⓳ rearrange: 〜を再配列する

⓴ end(ing) up with ...: 最後には〜が残る

㉑ arrest: 逮捕

㉒ beginning, intermediate, and advanced: 初級、中級、上級の

nights a week. For twenty-five years, he had taught his students millions of ❶vocabulary words. He had ❷patiently explained to them ❸the intricacies of English grammar, ❹complete with ❺built-in inconsistencies. He had even given them English poems and
5 short stories (written by himself and the more advanced students) to read. When ❻interrogated at the police station, however, our English teacher ❼proved ignorant of the most basic knowledge of the language. He did not know the ❽verb "to be" or "to do." He did not know there is ❾a past tense in English. He had never heard
10 of Shakespeare and ❿was not even aware that Australians and Englishmen also speak English.

In Ho Muoi's ⓫made-up English, there are not five but twenty-four ⓬vowels. The new ⓭nuances in ⓮pronunciation ⓯force each student to ⓰fine-tune his ear to the level of the finest musician.
15 ⓱There is a vast vocabulary for pain and bamboo but no ⓲equivalent for cheese. Any ⓳adjective can be used as a verb. *I will hot you*, for example, or, *Don't red me.* There are so many ⓴personal

---

❶ vocabulary: 語彙

❷ patiently: 根気よく

❸ the intricacies: 複雑さ

❹ complete with ...: 〜も含めた、揃えた

❺ built-in inconsistencies: あらかじめ組み込まれたいろんな矛盾

❻ interrogate(d): 〜を尋問する

❼ prove(d): 〜であることがわかる

❽ (a) verb: 動詞

❾ a past tense: 過去時制というもの

❿ was not even aware that ...: 〜ということすら認識していなかった

⓫ made-up: でっち上げの

⓬ vowel(s): 母音

を生徒たちに教え込み、英文法の複雑さを、元々組み込まれている矛盾もちゃんと含めて、辛抱強く説明した。英語の詩や短篇小説を授業で読ませさえした（作者は彼自身と上級クラスの生徒たち）。ところが、警察署で取り調べを受けてみると、我らが英語教師は、英語という言語のごく基礎的な知識すら持っていないことが判明した。be 動詞も知らなかったし、do も知らない。英語に過去時制があることも彼は知らなかった。シェークスピアという名も聞いたこともなかったし、オーストラリア人やイギリス人も英語を話すという事実も認識していなかった。

　ホー・ムオイの作り物の英語にあっては、母音は5つではなく24ある。発音はきわめて微妙な陰影に富み、生徒はみなそれら慣れぬ音を相手に、超一流の音楽家のレベルにまで耳を精緻にせねばならない。痛みと竹についての語彙は膨大であるが、チーズに当たる単語はない。形容詞はすべて動詞として使うことができる。I will hot you（私はあなたを熱いするでしょう）とか Don't red me（私を赤するな）といったふうに。代名詞はものすごく多く、

⓫ nuance(s): 微妙な違い

⓮ pronunciation: 発音

⓯ force: （〜することを）強いる

⓰ fine-tune: 〜を細かく調整する

⓱ There is a vast vocabulary for pain and bamboo ...: 痛みと竹に関する語彙が異様に多い。イヌイットは雪の白さを表わし分ける言葉をいくつも持っていることなどを例に、人の認識は言語に左右される、と唱えた「サピア＝ウォーフの仮説」に通じる発想。

⓲ (an) equivalent for ...: 〜に相当する語

⓳ (an) adjective: 形容詞

⓴ personal pronoun(s): 人称代名詞

pronouns, each one ❶denoting an exact relationship between speaker and ❷subject, that ❸even the most brilliant student cannot master them all.

❹By sheer coincidence, some of Ho Muoi's made-up English
5 words ❺correspond exactly with actual English. In his system, a cat is also called a cat; a tractor, a tractor; and ❻a rose, inevitably, perhaps, a rose.

❼Some of his more curious inventions ❽include *blanket*, to denote a husband. ❾*Basin*, to denote a wife. ❿*Pin prick*: a son. ⓫*A
10 leaky faucet*: a daughter.

Ho Muoi's ⓬delusion was so ⓭absolute, however, that after he ⓮was sentenced to twenty-five years for "⓯defrauding the people," he asked to be allowed to take to prison a "Dictionary of the English Language" and a "Dictionary of English Slang," two
15 ⓰volumes he himself had ⓱compiled, so that "I can continue my life studies."

---

❶ denoting <denote: 〜を示す
❷ subject: 対象、相手
❸ even the most brilliant student cannot master them all: どんなに優秀な学生でもすべてはマスターできない。日本語の人称代名詞の複雑さは、この記述からさほどかけ離れてもいない気もする。
❹ By sheer coincidence: まったくの偶然により
❺ correspond exactly with ...: 〜とぴったり一致する
❻ a rose, inevitably, perhaps, a rose: バラは、おそらく不可避的に、バラである。「おそらく不可避的」というのは、ガートルード・スタインの詩 "Sacred Emily" (1913) の中の有名な一文 "Rose is a rose is a rose is a rose." を踏まえているから。
❼ Some of his more curious inventions: 彼の捏造の中でも、より奇怪な部類に属す例

それら一つひとつが話者と相手との関係のありようを厳密に反映しているため、どんなに優秀な生徒でもすべてをマスターすることは不可能である。

　まったくの偶然によって、ホー・ムオイの作り物の英単語のいくつかは実際の英語とぴったり一致している。彼の体系にあっても、猫はやはり cat であり、トラククーは tractor、そしてバラも、おそらくは避けがたくと言うべきであろう、rose である。

　奇異な捏造例をいくつか挙げるなら、blanket（毛布）は夫を指し、basin（たらい）は妻を指す。pin prick（苛立たしいもの）は息子であり、a leaky faucet（水漏れする蛇口）は娘である。

　しかし、ホー・ムオイの妄想はあくまでも堅牢であった。「人民を搾取した」罪で禁固 25 年の刑を宣告されたときも、「生涯の研究を続けられるように」と、自ら編纂した二冊の辞書『英語辞典』『英語俗語辞典』を監獄に持ち込む許可を求めたのである。

❽ include:「〜を含む」と訳すより、「……としては〜などがある」と訳すとよい場合も多い。

❾ (a) Basin: たらい

❿ Pin prick: 針で空けた（ように小さい）穴、ちょっとした鬱陶しいこと

⓫ A leaky faucet: 水漏れする蛇口

⓬ delusion: 妄想

⓭ absolute: 絶対的な、完全な

⓮ was sentenced to ...: 〜の刑に処された

⓯ defraud(ing): 〜を詐取する

⓰ volume(s): 巻

⓱ compile(d): 〜を編纂する

It is ❶rumored that many of his ❷former students ❸have banded together to continue their English lessons. ❹Harassed by the police, they must ❺hold their nightly meetings in ❻underground bunkers, lit by oil lamps. Their strange ❼syllables, carried by the ❽erratic
5 winds, ❾crosshatch ❿the surrounding countryside.

But why are they doing this? You ask. Don't they know they are studying a false language?

As the universal language—⓫for now—English ⓬represents to these students the rest of the world. English *is* the world. These
10 students also know that ⓭Vietnam, as it exists, ⓮is not of this world. To ⓯cling even to a false English is to insist on another reality.

A ⓰bogus English is better than no English, is better, in fact, than actual English, since it corresponds to no English or American
15 reality.

Hoo he hoo ah utta ma nut m pap m home.

---

❶ rumor(ed): 〜と噂する
❷ former: 以前の
❸ have banded together: 団結している
❹ Harassed by: 〜に迫害されて
❺ hold: （会合などを）開く
❻ underground bunkers: 地下のシェルター
❼ syllable(s): 音節
❽ erratic: 不規則な
❾ crosshatch: 〜に網目の陰影をつける
❿ the surrounding countryside: 周囲の田園地帯
⓫ for now: いまのところは。英語はいつの世でも世界の共通語だったわけではもちろんない。たとえば中世ヨーロッパでの共通言語といえばラテン語だった。

　噂によれば、元生徒の多くが結束して英語のレッスンを続けているという。警察に妨害されるため、毎夜の集会は、石油ランプを灯した地下の隠れ家で開かねばならない。彼らの発する奇妙な音が、方向の定まらぬ風に乗って、近隣の田園を網目状の陰影で包む。

　でもなんでそんなことやってるんだ？　とあなたは問うだろう。知らないのか、自分たちが偽の言語を勉強してるってこと？

　普遍的な（いまのところは）言語として、英語はこれら生徒にとって自分たちの外の世界を体現している。英語こそ世界そのものなのだ。そしてこれらの生徒たちは、いま存在しているベトナムが、その世界に入っていないことを知っている。偽の英語であっても、それにしがみつくことは、もうひとつの現実の存在を主張することなのだ。

　インチキの英語でも、英語なしよりはいい。いや実際、本当の英語よりいいくらいだ——それはイギリスだのアメリカだのの現実なんかに対応していないのだから。

　フー・ヒー・フー・アー・アタ・マ・ナト・ム・パプ・ム・ホーム。

❶❷ represent(s): 〜を表わす、象徴している
❶❸ Vietnam, as it exists: いま存在しているベトナムは
❶❹ is not of this world: この世界の一部でない、この世界に属さない
❶❺ cling even to <cling to ...: 〜にしがみつく
❶❻ bogus: 偽の、いんちきの

●

ちなみに

　リン・ディンをアメリカでいち早く評価したのは作家マシュー・シャープ（Matthew Sharpe）である。2004年にシャープが行なったインタビューで、ディンは次のように言っている。"Americans judge the rest of the world by American standards and see failures everywhere. Which is I think preposterous. That's not how it is. Well, it's sort of how it is. (*They Laugh*.)"（アメリカ人はアメリカを基準にして世界を判断して、そこらじゅうに失敗や不足を見る。そういうのは馬鹿げてると思う。そういうもんじゃないだろう。てゆうか、まあちょっとそういうもんなんだけどさ。〔二人笑う〕。）——アメリカを叩きつつ、非アメリカ的なものを謳い上げて終わりもしないこの書き手らしい物言いである。

The Dysfunctional Family
Agnes Owens

機能不全家族

アグネス・オーエンズ

難易度 1
★ ☆ ☆

アグネス・オーエンズ
(Agnes Owens, 1926-2014)

　スコットランドの作家。1970 年代後半、50 代に入ってから創作教室に通いはじめ、アラスター・グレイ、ジェームズ・ケルマンといったスコットランドの重要作家たちの目にとまる。二度結婚し、さまざまな職に携わりながら七人の子供を育てた体験を素材に、労働者階級の生活を暴力的なまでに赤裸々に、かつ黒いユーモアとともに描くその作品は、*The Complete Short Stories* (2008) と *The Complete Novellas* (2009) ですべて読むことができる。

According to a neighbour in the ❷flat below we were a ❸dysfunctional family, though I wasn't sure what dysfunctional meant. I sometimes thought it meant we didn't wash enough. My young brother usually had ❹tide marks of dirt ❺up his
5 arms and sometimes I had them. Or perhaps it meant my mother ❻went around all day without stockings.

'I don't like them,' she'd say, 'they make my legs itch.'

I didn't like the sight of her bare legs with ❼ugly blue veins showing ❽where she sat too close to the fire; otherwise they were
10 fat and white, like lard. I told her to wear long skirts but she said bare legs gave her a feeling of freedom. Then Albie, my older brother, was ❾doing time for ❿holding up ⓫an old-age pensioner with a toy pistol. Was he dysfunctional? Or ⓬my Da? ⓭He got drunk every Friday so we had to walk the streets until he fell
15 asleep in the big room chair, otherwise he became very violent. I was the ⓮in-between sister and didn't think I did much to make the family dysfunctional, but never ⓯definitely knew, ⓰not being

❶ According to: 〜によれば、〜が言うには

❷ (a) flat: アパートやマンションの一世帯分を、イギリスでは flat、アメリカでは apartment という。a neighbour in the flat below は「自分たちの下の階に住んでいる人」ということになる。

❸ dysfunctional: 特に family という語と一緒に使われることが多い。a dysfunctional family で「機能不全家族」。語り手は小学生であり、しかも決して優等生でもなく、明らかにこの言葉の意味をわからずに使っている。

❹ tide mark(s): 本来は潮が引いたあとに海岸に残る筋のことを言うが、バスタブに残る湯垢の線を指したりもする。ここではさらに意味が広がって、体についた垢や泥の筋のことを言っている。

❺ up his arms: 腕の上の方に

❻ went around all day without stockings: 一日じゅうストッキングをはかず、ことさらに「動き回った」というよりは単にそうやって一日過ごした、という感じ。

アパートの下の階の人に言わせるとうちは機能不全家族だってことだった
けど、機能不全ってどういう意味かあたしにはよくわからなかった。体をあ
んまり洗わないってことかな、と思ったりもした。弟はたいてい、泥が両腕
に潮の跡みたいについてたし、あたしもときどきそうだった。それとも、う
ちの母さんが一日中ストッキングをはかずに過ごしてることだろうか。
「ストッキング、嫌なのよ」と母さんは言った。「脚がムズムズするから」

　でも母さんのむき出しの脚を見させられるのはこっちだって嫌だった。暖
炉のそばに座りすぎたところが、醜い青い血管までくっきり見えた。そうで
ないところは、ラードみたいに白くぼてっとしてる。長いスカートはいてよ、
とあたしは母さんに言ったけど、脚を出してる方が自由を感じるのよと母さ
んは言った。そのころ兄貴のオルビーは、老齢年金で暮らしてる人をおも
ちゃのピストルで脅して金を奪った罪で刑務所に入っていた。オルビーは機
能不全だろうか？　じゃなけりゃ父さんは？　父さんは毎週金曜に酔っ払う
ので、あたしたちは父さんが大部屋の椅子で寝入ってしまうまで外でうろう
ろしてないといけなかった。そうしないとすごく乱暴になるのだ。あたしは
兄と弟にはさまれた真ん中の子で、うちを機能不全にするようなことはそん
なにやってないと思ったけど、とにかくどういう意味かよくわからないので、

❼ ugly blue veins showing: 醜い青い血管が見えていて
❽ where she sat too close to the fire: 暖炉に近く座りすぎたあたりが
❾ doing time <do time: スラングで、「刑期を務める」「ムショで過ごす」
❿ hold(ing) up ...: 誰かにピストルを突きつけて金などを出させること。"holdup"
　 と名詞にしても使う。
⓫ an old-age pensioner <old-age pension: 老齢年金
⓬ my Da: あたしのとうさん。Dad 以上にくだけた感じ。
⓭ He got drunk every Friday: 金曜日には失業手当が支給されるから。
⓮ in-between: 中間の、あいだに入る
⓯ definitely: はっきりと
⓰ not being sure ...: because I wasn't sure ...

sure of what the word meant. **❶**A social worker visited us when Albie was **❷**in jail. I and my younger brother **❸**were ushered out of the room and pressed our ears to the door to hear **❹**what was going on. My mother came out smiling.

5 **❺**'What do you think?' she said. '**❻**Albie's being let out for **❼**good behaviour.'

Da said, 'How did they **❽**figure that out? He's never had a moment's good behaviour since the day he was born.'

'Just **❾**be nice to him,' said the social worker. 'Probably **❿**that's all he needs.'

10 Da gave her such **⓫**a look of disgust that I had to laugh.

'**⓬**None of that **⓭**nonsense from you, **⓮**miss!' said my mother, 'Albie has had a terrible time in jail, and don't forget he wasn't always **⓯**a criminal.'

15 'Does that mean he's dysfunctional?' I asked. She **⓰**glanced at me sharply.

---

❶ A social worker: ソーシャルワーカー、民生委員

❷ in jail: 刑務所に入っている

❸ were ushered out of the room: 部屋の外に連れ出された。usher: 〜を導く、案内する

❹ what was going on: what was happening

❺ 'What do you think?': 「ねえねえ聞いて」という感じ。

❻ Albie's being let out: Albie is being let out. let out ...: 〜を釈放する

❼ good behaviour: よい振る舞い、善行

❽ figure that out <figure out: （問題などを）解く、わかる。非常によく使う言い回し。p. 100, l. 15 にも出てきた。

❾ be nice to ...: 〜に優しくする

❿ that's all he needs: それが彼に必要なすべて＝彼に必要なのはそれだけ

はっきりとは言えなかった。オルビーが刑務所に入ってる最中にソーシャル
ワーカーがやって来た。あたしと弟は部屋から追い出されたので、二人で耳
をドアに押しつけて盗み聞きした。母さんがニコニコして部屋から出てきた。
「ねえねえ、オルビーがね、品行方正で釈放してもらえるんだって」

　父さんが言った。「そいつぁ不思議だな。あいつ、生まれてこのかた、品
行方正だったことなんていっぺんもないじゃねえか」

「とにかく優しくしてあげてくださいね」とソーシャルワーカーは言った。
「たぶんあの子に必要なのは優しさだけなんです」

　父さんが、さもうんざりした顔でソーシャルワーカーを見たので、あたし
は笑ってしまった。

「あんたにそんなこと言われたかないね！」と母さんがソーシャルワーカー
に言った。「あの子は刑務所でつらい目に遭ってきたんだし、それに忘れちゃ
困るよ、いつも犯罪者だったわけじゃないんだ」

「それって、オルビーは機能不全だってこと？」とあたしは訊いた。母さん
がぎろっとあたしを睨んだ。

⓫ a look of disgust: 嫌悪感をあらわにした、ふざけんじゃねえ、という感じの
表情。'disgust' 'disgusting' は嫌悪感を表わす際に大変よく使われる言葉。
⓬ None of that ...: ～なんかお断りだ
⓭ nonsense: たわごと、ばかげた考え
⓮ miss: 若い女性に対する呼びかけ。特に、名前を知らないときに使う。
⓯ a criminal: 犯罪者
⓰ glanced at me sharply: 怖い顔であたしをちらっと見た

'Where do you get ❶all these fancy words? ❷I hope you're not swearing.'

'It's a very good word,' said the social worker. '❸I bet your daughter will ❹turn out clever by the time she leaves school.'

5　'That'll be a surprise. She never goes there,' said my Da.

The social worker ❺hesitated ❻as if going to say something about that, then ❼shook her head and said, 'Good luck with Albie. I'll be back ❽to see how you're getting on.'

'Do that,' said my mother, and after the woman left added,

10 '❾Interfering ❿bitch.'

It was ⓫rotten for me when Albie came home. He lay in bed all the time smoking or ⓬snorting dope. ⓭Worse still it was my bed, so I had to sleep on the big-room couch until one day he got up early, washed and shaved without saying a word, then left the house

15 and was never seen again. At the evening meal mother ⓮started laying out a plate for him, though before that he had never come to the table. When the plate ⓯was emptied into the bin my Da said,

---

❶ all these fancy words: そんな気取った言葉。fancy は「お洒落な」の意だが、この場合のように悪意を込めて使うことも多い。

❷ I hope you're not swearing: それって汚い言葉使ってるんじゃないだろうね。swear は damn! Jesus! 等の汚い言葉（swear word）を口にすること。母親は dysfunctional という言葉をまったく知らず、swear word かもしれないと思っている。

❸ I bet: I'm sure

❹ turn out: 結果として～になる、大きくなって～になる

❺ hesitate(d): ためらう

❻ as if going to say ...: as if she were going to say ...

❼ shook her head <shake one's head: 首を横に振ること。否定的な気持ちの

「あんた、そんな気どった言葉どこで覚えるんだい？　それって汚い言葉じゃないんだろうね」

「すごくいい言葉ですよ」とソーシャルワーカーが言った。「お嬢さん、学校を卒業なさるころにはきっとさぞ賢くなってらっしゃいますよ」

「そうなったらビックリだね。こいつ、学校なんて全然行かないんだから」と父さんが言った。

　それについて何か言おうとするみたいにソーシャルワーカーは迷ってたけど、結局首を横に振るだけで、「オルビー、うまく行きますように。またそのうち様子を見に伺いますから」と言った。

「そうしてくださいな」と母さんは言って、相手がいなくなってから、「お節介な女だよ」と言い足した。

　オルビーが帰ってくると、あたしはひどいことになった。何しろオルビーは一日中ベッドに寝転がって、煙草を喫ったり、ドラッグをやったりしている。なお悪いことに、それはあたしのベッドで、あたしは大きい部屋のカウチで寝ないといけなかった。やがてある日、オルビーは早起きして、何も言わずに体を洗ってヒゲを剃って、家を出て、それっきり帰ってこなかった。晩ご飯の食卓に、母さんはオルビーの席を用意するようになったけど、実はいたときだって食卓になんか来たことなかったのだ。オルビーの分がゴミ入

表現。

❽ to see how you're getting on: あなたがたがどうやっているか見に＝様子を見に

❾ Interfering: お節介な

❿ (a) bitch: 女性を罵って言う言葉。

⓫ rotten: 不快な , ひどい

⓬ snorting dope: snort は鼻から dope（ドラッグ）を吸うこと。

⓭ Worse still: もっと悪いことに

⓮ started laying out a plate: 皿を出すようになった。started ...ing は「〜しはじめた」でもいいが「〜するようになった」と訳すとしっくり来ることが多い。

⓯ was emptied into the bin: ゴミ入れに空けられた

'❶A waste of good food,' though none of us would have eaten it
❷anyway. I had never liked my older brother but became so bored
that I wished he'd come home and ❸liven things up. When he was
here you never knew when ❹the cops would ❺come to the door
5 because he'd done something. At school I had written a story
about him for ❻a composition, ❼making him out to be ❽wrongly
accused of stealing money by a ❾spiteful old-age pensioner. The
teacher said ❿this was not the kind of story she wanted and put
⓫a big cross through it. I was so angry I ⓬stayed off until ⓭the
10 school board came to the door ⓮threatening Da with a fine.
⓯Between one thing and another we at last forgot all about Albie
except my mother, who sometimes said he might have gone to
Australia to live with a cousin of hers who had a sheep farm. Da
said that was ⓰unlikely, since Australia would not ⓱let in a boy
15 who could hardly write his own name.

Our house was in a long ⓲terrace built a century ago and
owned by ⓳the council because ⓴the landlord had ㉑abandoned it.

---

❶ A waste of …: ～の無駄

❷ anyway: どのみち

❸ liven things up: 場を盛り上げる

❹ the cops <a cop: 警官、おまわり

❺ come to the door: 玄関に来る、うちへ訪ねてくる

❻ a composition: 作文

❼ making him out to be <make out …: ～に見せかける。*He makes himself
  out to be an expert but he knows nothing about it.* (エキスパートみたい
  なふりしてるけど実は何も知らない)

❽ wrongly accused of …: ～をしたと不当に非難されて

❾ spiteful: 意地の悪い

❿ this was not the kind of story she wanted: これは彼女が求めているたぐ

れに空けられると、父さんは「もったいない、せっかくの食べ物が」と言ったけど、どのみち誰も食べやしなかっただろう。オルビーのこと、あたしは好きだったことなんかなかったけど、あんまり退屈なので、帰ってきて少しはにぎやかにしてくれないかと思った。オルビーがうちにいると、しょっちゅう何かしでかすから、いつ警官がうちに来るかわからないのだ。学校であたしは、オルビーのことを作文に書いて、意地悪な年寄りの年金生活者から、金を奪ったと不当な非難を受けた人物に描いた。こんなの書けなんて言ってませんよと先生は言って、あたしの作文に大きな×をつけた。あたしはすごく頭に来て、学校に行かなくなって、そのうち教育委員会がうちに来て、罰金を払わせますよと父さんを脅かした。そんなこんなで、みんなやがてオルビーのことは忘れてしまったけど、母さんだけは別で、あの子はオーストラリアに行ったかもしれないねえ、母さんのいとこがあっちで羊の飼育やってるからねえ、なんて言ったりした。でも父さんは、それはないんじゃないかね、自分の名前もろくすっぽ書けない奴をオーストラリアが入れてくれるとは思えないね、と言った。

　うちは一世紀前に建てられた長屋の一部で、持ち主が放棄したので市の持

いの話ではなかった＝こういうものを書けとは言わなかった

⓫ a big cross: 大きなバツ

⓬ stayed off: （学校に）行かなかった

⓭ the school board: 教育委員会

⓮ threaten(ing) Da with a fine: 罰金を払わせるぞと父さんを脅す

⓯ Between one thing and another: そんなこんなで

⓰ unlikely: ありそうにない

⓱ let in ...: 〜を入国させる

⓲ (a) terrace: 何軒かつながった長屋式住宅

⓳ the council: （市や町の）議会、自治体

⓴ the landlord: 家主

㉑ abandon(ed): 〜を放棄する

The roof **❶**leaked into the big room, as we called it, and the toilet needed **❷**fixing, but we couldn't **❸**get the council to do repairs as my mother **❹**hardly ever paid **❺**the rent. But I liked living here because the terrace **❻**had big green fields behind where cows ⁵**❼**roamed at leisure and we **❽**had tons of room to play. My young brother would **❾**lie flat on his stomach and pretend to shoot at the animals with a toy gun he got for Christmas, while I played at **❿**peever on **⓫**the cobblestone side lane with my **⓬**trashy friends who seldom washed or went to school either. But **⓭**gradually they ¹⁰all left for **⓮**the new council flats and we were the last to go. After Albie left, the big **⓯**snag in our lives was our Da. When drunk on Fridays he **⓰**became increasingly violent so we **⓱**took to hiding in the old **⓲**washhouses. This was fine in summer after we **⓳**dragged in mattresses to sleep on but we **⓴**dreaded the coming of winter ¹⁵when it would be too cold to do that. But **㉑**by a great stroke of luck

---

❶ leak(ed): (容器や屋根などが) 漏る
❷ fix(ing): 〜を修理する
❸ get the council to do repairs: 市議会に修理をやってもらう
❹ hardly ever: almost never
❺ the rent: 家賃
❻ had big green fields behind: 裏に広い緑の野原があった
❼ roam(ed) at leisure: のんびりさまよう
❽ had tons of room to play: 遊ぶ場所はたっぷりあった。tons of: plenty of. 'room' は「部屋」ではなく「空間」「場所」。
❾ lie flat on his stomach: 腹を下にして平たく横たわる＝腹ばいになる
❿ peever: スコットランド英語で「石けり」
⓫ the cobblestone side lane: 石畳の裏道
⓬ trashy: クズみたいな

ち物になっていた。大部屋、とみんな呼んでいた部屋は雨漏りがしたし、トイレも修理が必要だったけど、家賃をろくに払わないので直してくれと市に頼んでもやってくれなかった。でもここに住むのがあたしは好きだった。裏は広い野原で、牛がのんびりうろついて、あたしたちの遊ぶ場所もたっぷりあった。弟はべったり腹ばいになって、クリスマスに買ってもらったおもちゃの銃で動物を撃つ真似をし、あたしはあたしで、ろくに体も洗わず学校にも行かないクズの友だちと一緒に石畳の路地で石蹴りをして遊んだ。でもみんな徐々に、市が新しく建てたアパートに越していって、最後にはうちの家族しか残らなかった。オルビーがいなくなると、うちの暮らしで最大の厄介は父さんになった。金曜日に酔っ払うと、ますます乱暴になってきたので、あたしたちは古い洗濯場に隠れるようになった。夏はそこへマットレスを持っていって寝ればいいので問題なかったけど、寒くなったらそんなことできないので、冬が来るのがあたしたちは心配だった。でも、すごくいい具合に、

❸ gradually: だんだんと
❹ the new council flats: 新しい市営のアパート
❺ (a) snag: 障害、厄介
❻ became increasingly violent: ますます乱暴がひどくなった
❼ took to hiding <take to ...ing: ～するのが習慣になった、～するようになった
❽ washhouse(s): 洗濯場
❾ drag(ged) in ...: ～を引きずり入れる
⓴ dread(ed): ～を恐れる
㉑ by a great stroke of luck: 思わぬ幸運で。stroke は幸運などの「到来」。

Da **❶**snuffed it from drinking too much. **❷**Mind you, I cried about that. His violent nature **❸**was worsened by alcohol but still, he was our Da and not too bad to us when **❹** sober. Then next thing was mother **❺**taking to her bed with a bottle of **❻**Graham's port that she
5 kept under the pillow. She would say, 'Your poor Da, **❼**how I miss him,' and give me and my young brother **❽**a sip of it, after which he'd **❾**be sick on the carpet and I'd have to clean it up.

'Don't hit that child,' my mother would say when I **❿**made to **⓫**slap him. 'He's an **⓬**orphan and **⓭**the more to be pitied.'

10 This infuriated me for I was the only one who missed Da so I was **⓮**even more to be pitied. Then one day, as if by a miracle, my mother got out of bed and **⓯**poured the Graham's port down the sink, **⓰** tidied herself up and said she was going to look for a job because she **⓱**was fed up with living **⓲**on the dole and being **⓳**the
15 talk of the street.

'That's great,' I said. 'What time will you be home at? I'll have the dinner ready.'

---

❶ snuff(ed) it: スラングで「死ぬ」「くたばる」。父親の突然の死を語るこの一文のあっけらかんとした感じがこの作家の真骨頂。
❷ Mind you: いいかい、よく聞いてよ
❸ was worsened by alcohol: アルコールで余計ひどくなった
❹ sober: しらふの
❺ taking to her bed: ベッドに入り浸りになって
❻ Graham's port: よく知られたブランドのポートワイン。Graham の発音は「グラハム」ではなく「グレアム」。
❼ how I miss him: 彼がいなくて何と寂しいことか
❽ a sip: ひと口
❾ be sick: 吐く
❿ made to <make to ...: 〜しようとする

お酒を飲み過ぎたせいで父さんは死んでしまった。そりゃあたしも、いち おう涙は流した。もともと乱暴な性格がお酒のせいでますますひどくなった けれど、とにかくあたしたちの父さんだったのだし、しらふのときはそこま でひどくなかったのだ。そしたら今度は母さんが、グレアム・ポートワイン を枕の下に隠して一日中ベッドで過ごすようになった。「父さん可哀想にね え、いなくなって寂しいよ」と母さんは言って、あたしと弟にも一口飲ませ てくれて、そしたら弟が絨毯にゲロを吐いて、あたしが掃除しないといけな かった。

「ぶっちゃ駄目だよ」と母さんは、あたしが弟をひっぱたこうとするのを見 て言った。「この子はもうみなし子の、可哀想な身なんだからね」

　そう言われてあたしはすごく頭に来た。父さんがいなくなって寂しがって るのはあたしだけであって、あたしの方がもっと可哀想なのだ。やがてある 日、奇跡のように、母さんがベッドから出て、グレアム・ポートワインの中 身を流しに空けて、身だしなみを整え、職を探しに行くと宣言した。失業年 金で暮らしてあれこれ噂されるのはもううんざりだよ、と母さんは言った。

「すごいねえ」とあたしは言った。「何時に帰ってくるの？　晩ご飯、用意 しとくよ」

⓫ slap: 〜をひっぱたく
⓬ orphan: みなし子。母親はまだいるのだから厳密には正しくない。
⓭ the more to be pitied: その分いっそう哀れまれるべき
⓮ even more: もっといっそう
⓯ poured the Graham's port down the sink: グレアムのポートワインを流し に捨てた
⓰ tidied herself up <tidy oneself up: 自分を小ぎれいにする＝身づくろいする
⓱ was fed up with ...: 〜にうんざりした
⓲ on the dole: 失業手当に頼って。イギリスでは非常によく耳にする言い方。
⓳ the talk of the street: 街の噂、噂の種

'I don't know,' she said, and that's when I began to worry.

'❶You're not leaving us?' I said. 'I wouldn't know how to ❷take care of things.'

'You'll learn,' she said and we ❸never heard of her again. I
5 might have ❹cried my eyes out if I'd known she wasn't coming back. It ❺dawned on us gradually, though it was a terrible thing to happen. Luckily she had left ❻the Family Allowance Book on the mantelpiece ❼which got us food for the week if I was careful. On Saturdays ❽me and my young brother would go for a walk round
10 ❾the duck pond and throw them ❿crusts we didn't want from our bread, especially the black crusts. I believe we were quite happy then, though it's hard to imagine that now.

But things never went ⓫smoothly for us. ⓬Not long after that a social worker came to the door, ⓭the one who'd come about Albie,
15 and asked why I was not at school. I don't think she believed me when I said mother ⓮had gone off to find work and I had to look after my younger brother.

---

❶ You're not leaving us?: leave 〜と言うと、原則として、単に一時的に置いて いくのではなく、捨てて出ていく、という意味合いがはっきりある。

❷ take care of things: いろんなことに対処する

❸ never heard of her again: 以後二度と噂も聞かなかった

❹ cried my eyes out <cry one's eyes out: おいおい泣く、泣きはらす。p. 22, l. 9 と同じ。

❺ dawned on us gradually: じわじわ少しずつわかってきた

❻ the Family Allowance Book: 家族手当手帳

❼ which got us food for the week: それでその週の食べ物は手に入った

❽ me and my young brother: 上流階級なら my younger brother and I とで も言うところ。

❾ the duck pond: アヒル池

「うーん、どうかしらねえ」と母さんは言って、それであたしは心配になってきた。

「あたしたちのこと、置いてくんじゃないよね？」とあたしは言った。「あたし、一人じゃどうしたらいいかわかんないよ」

「じきわかるって」と母さんは言って、それっきり噂すら聞かなかった。もう帰ってこないとはじめから承知してたら、あたしとしてもわあわあ泣いただろうと思う。ものすごくひどい話だったけど、すぐにはピンとこなくて、じわじわわかってきたのだ。幸い、家族手当手帳は炉棚に置きっぱなしだったから、気をつけて使えば毎週の食べ物は何とかなった。土曜日になるとあたしと弟はアヒル池へ散歩に行って、パンの残りの、要らないところ、特に黒く焦げたところを投げてやった。いまからは想像しづらいけど、あのころあたしたちはけっこう幸せだったと思う。

けれど、いつまでもうまくは行かなかった。それから間もなく、ソーシャルワーカーがうちに来た。オルビーのことで来たのと同じ人で、何であなたは学校に行っていないのかとあたしに訊いた。母さんが仕事を探しに行って、あたしが弟の面倒見なくちゃいけないんです、と答えたけど、きっと信じてなかったと思う。

---

❿ crust(s): パンの皮
⓫ smoothly: すんなりと
⓬ Not long after that: その後まもなく
⓭ the one who'd come about Albie: オルビーの件で前に来た人
⓮ had gone off to find work: 仕事を探しに出かけた

'When was that?' she said, maybe thinking I was talking about that morning. When I said two months her face **❶**took on an ominous look.

'Two months?' she **❷**shrieked. 'I've never heard of anything so
5 **❸**disgraceful. **❹**Get your coats on. You're coming with me.'

We both kicked and **❺**struggled and I believe I **❻**would have got the better of her if **❼**a strange man hadn't come in, **❽**got hold of us and pushed us into a van as if we were **❾**dogs being taken to the dog pound. My younger brother was **❿**yelling for my mother but I
10 said nothing. **⓫**I knew when I was beat. I never saw him again. All my family had gone and I **⓬**was left on my own.

They put me in a hostel for **⓭**wayward children and after a few months of that I **⓮**was fostered by a very nice middle-aged couple who gave me everything I wanted. **⓯**The snag was, I had to be
15 **⓰**obedient, well mannered, and **⓱**speak with a proper accent which was the hardest thing to do. Also I was allowed only to **⓲**befriend

---

❶ took on an ominous look: 険悪な表情になった。take on: （表情などを）帯びる

❷ shriek(ed): 金切り声を上げる

❸ disgraceful: ひどい、恥ずべき

❹ Get your coats on: コートを着なさい

❺ struggle(d): もがく、抵抗する

❻ would have got the better of <get the better of ...: ～を負かす

❼ a strange man: 見たこともない男。「不思議な男」ではない。

❽ got hold of us: あたしたちをつかまえた

❾ dogs being taken to the dog pound: 犬の収容所（pound）に連れていかれる犬たち

❿ yell(ing) for my mother: 母さぁん～とわめく

「探しに行ったって、いつのこと？」とソーシャルワーカーは訊いた。たぶん、けさとかの話だと思ったのだろう。二か月前、とあたしが言うと、顔が見るみる険悪になった。

「二か月？」とソーシャルワーカーは金切り声を上げた。「そんなひどい話、聞いたことありませんよ。あなたたち、コートを着なさい。一緒に来るのよ」

あたしたちはばたばた暴れて抵抗した。あれでもし、知らない男の人が入ってきたりしなかったら、何とか撃退できたと思う。でもその男があたしたちをつかまえて、収容所に犬を連れてくみたいにバンに押し込めた。弟は母さぁん〜とわめいてたけど、あたしは何も言わなかった。負けたら負けたと、あたしにはわかるのだ。それきり弟には二度と会わなかった。うちの家族はみんないなくなってしまって、あたしは一人残された。

不良の子供を収容する施設にあたしは入れられて、そこで何か月か過ごしたあと、すごく優しい中年夫婦に引きとられた。欲しい物は何でも買ってもらえた。問題は、言うことを聞かないといけない、お行儀よくしてないといけない、そして——これが一番つらい——正しい喋り方をしないといけないことだった。それに、大人しい、お行儀のいい女の子しか友だちにしちゃい

❶ I knew when I was beat: 私は負かされたときには（負けだと）わかった

❷ was left on my own: 一人取り残された

❸ wayward children: 言うことをきかない子供たち＝問題児

❹ was fostered by ...: 〜が養子にとってくれた

❺ The snag: p. 136, l. 11 と同じく「厄介」「問題」

❻ obedient, well mannered: 言うことを聞く、お行儀のいい

❼ speak with a proper accent: きちんとした喋り方をする。'accent' は「訛り」。イギリスにおいては訛りは（地域以上に）階級の問題であり時にほとんど人格の問題である。

❽ befriend: 〜と仲よくする

❶nice well-mannered girls, which I did **❷**without too much bother, but I **❸**swore to myself I would **❹**run away **❺**at the first opportunity to find my young brother. Once I **❻**came past our old home, half of it still standing, and it struck me it would be **❼**near impossible
5 to find him. He **❽**could be anywhere in the wide world, maybe even dead, so I **❾**held my peace and turned my head away **❿**but not before thinking I saw his face staring at me from **⓫**a cracked window pane. I knew it was my imagination, and **⓬**deep in my heart **⓭**by then I didn't want to find him, because I had changed so
10 much, and **⓮**the chances were he wouldn't have changed at all.

15

---

❶ nice: きちんとした

❷ without too much bother: そんなに苦労せずに

❸ swore <swear: 誓う

❹ run away: 家出する

❺ at the first opportunity: 最初のチャンスが訪れたらすぐ

❻ came past our old home: かつてみんなで住んでいた家の前を通った

❼ near impossible: ほとんど不可能（nearly impossible）

❽ could be anywhere: どこにいてもおかしくない

❾ held my peace <hold one's peace: 沈黙を保つ

❿ but not before ...: でもその前に〜した

⓫ a cracked window pane: ひびの入った窓ガラス

⓬ deep in my heart: 心の奥底で

けない。まあそれはあんまり考えずにそうしたけど、チャンスがあったらすぐ逃げ出して弟を探しに行くんだ、そうあたしは心に誓った。あるとき、かつてのあたしたちの家の前を通ったら、半分はまだ建っていた。あたしはふっと、弟を見つけるなんてほとんど不可能だ、と思った。この広い世界の、どこにいたっておかしくない。ひょっとしてもう死んじゃったかもしれない。だからあたしは何も言わず、目をそらしたけど、その直前、弟の顔が一瞬、ひび割れた窓ガラスの向こうからこっちをじっと見てる気がした。あたしの想像だとわかってはいたし、もうそのころあたしは、心の奥底では、弟を見つけたいとは思っていなかったのだ。なぜなら、あたしはこんなに変わってしまったのに、弟はたぶん全然変わっていないだろうから。

❸ by then: もうそのころには
❹ the chances were: たぶん〜だろうと思った（=It was likely that ...）

ちなみに

　最初の長篇小説を出してくれる出版社を見つけようと奮闘していた
とき、スコットランドの有名なコメディアンの推薦文でもあれば出し
てやる、と出版社に言われたオーエンズは、原稿を（コピーもとら
ずに！）ビリー・コノリーの家に送った。もちろん返事は来ず、原
稿を取り返すすべもなかった。が、やがて彼女は掃除婦の仕事に就
き、振り当てられた家の一軒がなんとコノリーの家で、掃除をして
いたら自分の原稿に行きあたった。取り戻した原稿はやがて 1984 年、
Gentlemen of the West として出版された。

The Finkelstein 5
Nana Kwame Adjei-Brenyah

ザ・フィンケルスティーン5
ナナ・クワメ・アジェイ＝ブレニヤー

難易度 3
★ ★ ★

ナナ・クワメ・アジェイ＝ブレニヤー
（Nana Kwame Adjei-Brenyah, 1991-　）

　ニューヨーク州生まれ。両親はガーナ系の移民。シラキュース大学で創作を学び、2018 年、ここで取り上げた "The Finkelstein 5" を巻頭作品とする短篇集 *Friday Black* で衝撃のデビューを果たす。人種問題と資本主義の破壊的側面を二大テーマとして、リアルな要素とシュールな要素を大胆に合体させた作品が多い。

F ela, the headless girl, walked toward Emmanuel. Her neck
❶jagged with red savagery. She was silent, but he could feel
her waiting for him to do something, anything.

Then his phone rang, and he woke up.

5 He took a deep breath and set **❷**the Blackness in his voice
down to a 1.5 **❸**on a 10-point scale. "Hi there, how are you doing
today? Yes, yes, **❹**I did recently inquire about the status of my
application. Well, all right, okay. Great to hear. I'll be there. **❺**Have
a spectacular day." Emmanuel rolled out of bed and brushed his
10 teeth. The house was quiet. His parents had already left for work.

That morning, like every morning, the first decision he made
❻regarded his Blackness. His skin was a deep, constant brown. In
public, when people could actually see him, it was impossible to
get his Blackness down to anywhere near a 1.5. If he wore a tie,
15 **❼**wing-tipped shoes, smiled constantly, used **❽**his indoor voice,
and **❾**kept his hands strapped and calm at his sides, he could get
his Blackness as low as 4.0.

---

❶ jagged with red savagery: 直訳すれば「赤い残虐行為でギザギザになって」。
その前に the headless girl という記述もあるので、どういうことかここです
でにある程度想像はつく。

❷ the Blackness: こういうものを数字で表わす習慣が現実にあるわけではない。
だがこの小説を読み進めていくなかで、そのリアルさはどんどん明らかになっ
ていく。

❸ on a 10-point scale: 10 段階で

❹ I did recently inquire about the status of my application: 直訳は「事実
私の応募の状態に関し最近問い合わせました」。非常にあらたまった、大人びた
言い方をしようとしている感じ。

❺ Have a spectacular day: "Have a good day" のもう少し大げさな言い方。

❻ regard(ed): 〜に関係する

　フェラが、首のない女の子が、イマニュエルの方に歩いてきた。首に赤い野蛮なギザギザが入っている。女の子は何も言わなかったが、彼が何かしてくれるのを、なんでもいいからしてくれるのを、待っているのがわかった。

　と、電話が鳴って、目が覚めた。

　深く息を吸って、声の黒人度を 10 段階の 1.5 まで下げた。「あどうも、お電話ありがとうございます。ええ、はい、応募の件の進み具合、先日お訊ねしました。あ、はい、承知しました。よかったです。伺います。どうぞ素晴らしい一日を」。イマニュエルはベッドから転がり降りて、歯を磨いた。家の中は静かだった。両親はすでに仕事に出かけている。

　その朝も、まず最初に下した決断は黒人度に関するものだった。肌は濃い、一定の茶色である。人前で、姿を実際に見られるところでは、黒人度を 1.5 あたりまで下げるのは不可能だ。ネクタイをして、ウィングチップの革靴を履いて、終始ニコニコして、屋内用の声を使い、両手を脇に縛りつけたみたいに大人しくさせておけば、まあ 4.0 ぐらいまでは落とせる。

❼ wing-tipped shoes: ウィングチップ・シューズ。爪先に翼型の模様がついた革靴。たぶんイマニュエルはふだんはもっとカジュアルな靴をはいている。

❽ his indoor voice: 室内用の声。これもべつにそういう言い方が普通にあるわけではない。主人公がつねに場所を考え、演技を強いられていることが、いろんな言い回しから示唆される。

❾ kept his hands strapped ... at his sides: 直訳すれば「両手を脇に縛りつけておいた」。こういう文脈で普通 strap という言葉は使わない。それだけ意志の力を行使しないといけない感じが伝わってくる。

Though Emmanuel was happy about ❶scoring the interview, he also felt ❷guilty about feeling happy about anything. Most people he knew were still ❸mourning the Finkelstein ❹verdict: after twenty-eight minutes of ❺deliberation, a ❻jury of his peers had ❼acquitted George Wilson Dunn ❽of any wrongdoing whatsoever. He had been ❾indicted for ❿allegedly using a chain saw to ⓫hack off the heads of five black children outside the Finkelstein Library in Valley Ridge, South Carolina. The court had ⓬ruled that because the children were basically ⓭loitering and not actually inside the library reading, ⓮as one might expect of productive members of society, it was reasonable that Dunn had felt threatened by these five black young people and, thus, he ⓯was well within his rights when he protected himself, his library-loaned DVDs, and his children by going into the back of his ⓰Ford F-150 and retrieving his ⓱Hawtech PRO eighteen-inch 48cc chain saw.

The case had seized the country by the ear and heart, and was

---

❶ scoring the interview: 面接にこぎつけたこと
❷ guilty: 罪悪感がある、疚<ruby>疚<rt>やま</rt></ruby>しい
❸ mourn(ing): 〜を嘆き悲しむ
❹ verdict: 評決
❺ deliberation: 審議
❻ jury of his peers: 直訳すれば「同等の地位の者たちから成る陪審」だが、この場合 peer は、普通の「年齢・社会層等が同じ者」という意味よりも広く、ほぼ "equal" に等しい。陪審を選ぶにあたって、特定の人種・階級・年齢に集中しないよう配慮したということだが、このあと語られる裁判で、それがどこまで実現されているか……。
❼ acquit(ted): 〜を無罪にする
❽ of any wrongdoing whatsoever: まったく何の犯罪に関しても (acquit A

面接が決まったのは嬉しかったが、嬉しい気持ちが疚しくもあった。知っている人間の大半は、フィンケルスティーン判決の結果をいまだ悼んでいる。28分の議論ののち、自分と同様の地位の人々から成る陪審によって、ジョージ・ウィルソン・ダンはいかなる罪も犯していない、と無罪放免されたのである。サウスキャロライナ州ヴァリー・リッジのフィンケルスティーン図書館の外で黒人の子供五人の首をチェーンソーでめった切りにした廉でダンは起訴されたのだった。裁決によれば、子供たちは要するに外でぶらぶらしていたのであって、社会の生産的成員に相応しく図書館のなかで本を読んでいたのではないから、これら五人の黒人にダンが脅威を感じたのも道理であって、したがって彼が、自分自身と、図書館で借りたDVDと、子供たちを護るために、フォードF-150の後部に行き、ホーテクPRO18インチ48ccのチェーンソーを持ち出したことは十分に権利の範囲内であった、ということなのだ。

　裁判は全米の耳と心をとらえ、いまだにどこでもこの話題で持ち切りだっ

❾ indict(ed): 〜を起訴、告発する
❿ allegedly:（真偽はともかく）申し立てによれば
⓫ hack off ...: 〜をめった切りにする
⓬ rule(d) that ...: 〜という判決を下す
⓭ loiter(ing): ぶらつく、たむろする
⓮ as one might expect of productive members of society: 社会の生産的成員に人が期待するとおりに
⓯ was well within his rights: 十分権利の範囲内だった
⓰ Ford F-150: ごく一般的な型のトラック。
⓱ Hawtech PRO ... chain saw: 架空の商品だが、いかにもチェーンソーらしい記述が並ぶ。

still, mostly, the only thing anyone was talking about. Finkelstein
❶became the news cycle. On one side of the broadcast world,
❷anchors openly wept for the children, who were saints in their
eyes; on the opposite side were personalities like❸Brent Kogan, the
5 ❹ever gruff and opinionated host of *What's the Big Deal?*, who had
said during an online panel discussion, "Yes, yes, they were kids,
❺but also, fuck niggers." Most ❻news outlets ❼fell somewhere in
between.

On verdict day, Emmanuel's family and friends of many
10 different races and backgrounds had gathered together and
watched a television tuned to a station that had sympathized with
the children, who were popularly known as the Finkelstein Five.
Pizza and drinks were served. When the ruling was announced,
Emmanuel ❽felt a clicking and grinding in his chest. It burned. His
15 mother, known to be one of the liveliest and happiest women in
the neighborhood, threw a plastic cup filled with Coke across the
room. When the plastic fell and the soda ❾splattered, the people
stared at Emmanuel's mother. Seeing Mrs. Gyan that way meant

---

❶ became the news cycle: 日々報道された
❷ anchor(s): キャスター
❸ Brent Kogan, ... host of *What's the Big Deal?*: パーソナリティ名も番組名
  も架空。What's ... は「それがどうした？」「何をそんなに騒いでいるのか？」
  といった意で、世間で話題になっていることを取り上げる、という響きのある
  番組名。
❹ ever gruff and opinionated: つねにぶっきらぼうで独断的な
❺ but also ...: この発言でこの人物の人種観は明らか。n...s は現在、（黒人以外が）
  やすやす口にできる言葉ではない。
❻ news outlet(s): ニュース機関、放送局

た。フィンケルスティーンはニュースの中心となった。放送界の一方の側では、子供たちは聖者であり、キャスターたちは彼らを悼んで大っぴらに泣いた。だがもう一方では、ブレント・コーガンのようなパーソナリティもいた——人気番組『それがどうした』のホストを務める、粗野で独断的なこの人物は、ネット上で行なわれたパネル・ディスカッションで、「ええ、そりゃたしかに子供でしたよ、だけどその、ニガーなわけでしょう」と言ったのである。大半のニュースは、この両極端のあいだのどこかに位置していた。

　判決が下った日、イマニュエルは家族とともに、人種も背景もさまざまな友人たちと一緒に集まって、いまやフィンケルスティーン・ファイブとして広く知られるに至った子供たちに共感を寄せている局の放送を観た。ピザと飲み物が出された。判決結果が発表されると、イマニュエルは胸の中がカチッ、ギリギリと締めつけられるのを感じた。胸が燃えるように熱かった。この界隈の誰よりも生きいきとしていて誰よりも陽気で通っている彼の母親が、コーラの入ったプラスチックのカップを部屋の向こうに投げつけた。カップが落ちてコーラが飛び散ると、人々は呆然とイマニュエルの母親を見た。ミセス・ジアンがこんなふうにふるまうということは、これは本当なの

---

❼ fell somewhere in between: だいたいそのあいだのどこかに位置した
❽ felt a clicking and grinding in his chest: 胸にカチッ（clicking）、ギリギリ（grinding）という締め付けを感じた。この後くり返し出てくる重要なイメージ。
❾ splatter(ed): ビシャッと飛び散る

it was real: they'd lost. Emmanuel's father walked away from the
group wiping his eyes, and Emmanuel felt the grinding in his chest
❶settle to a cold nothingness. On the ride home, his father ❷cursed.
His mother ❸punched honks out of the steering wheel. Emmanuel
5 ❹breathed in and watched his hands appear, then disappear, then
appear, then disappear as they rode past streetlights. He ❺let the
nothing he was feeling wash over him ❻in one cold wave after
another.

But now that he'd ❼been called in for an interview with ❽Stich's,
10 a store ❾self-described as an "❿innovator with a classic sensibility"
that specialized in vintage sweaters, Emmanuel had something to
think about besides the bodies of those kids, ⓫severed at the neck,
growing damp in ⓬ thick, pulsing, shooting blood. Instead, he
thought about what to wear.

15 In a vague ⓭move of solidarity, Emmanuel ⓮climbed into
the loose-fitting ⓯cargoes he'd worn on a camping trip. Then he

---

❶ settle to ...: ～に定着する、落着く
❷ curse(d): 悪態をつく
❸ punched honks out of the steering wheel: ハンドルのクラクションを何
　度も叩いた（「ハンドル」は和製英語で、英語では p. 54, 註❺で見たとおり
　steering wheel）。
❹ breathed in: 息を吸い込んだ
❺ let the nothing he was feeling wash over him: 直訳は「自分が感じている
　無が、自分の上を波のように流れていくままにした」。
❻ in one cold wave after another: 冷たい波となって次々に
❼ be(en) called in for an interview: 面接に呼ばれる
❽ Stich's: t を足して stitch とすれば「縫う」「縫い」の意なので、いかにもアパ
　レルの店の名前っぽい。

だ——彼らは負けたのだ。イマニュエルの父親は目の涙を拭いながら人の輪から歩き去り、イマニュエルは胸のギリギリが冷たい虚無へと落着くのを感じた。家への帰り道、父は悪態をついた。母は何度もクラクションを思いきり叩いた。イマニュエルは息を吸い込んで、街灯を通り過ぎるとともに自分の両手が現われ、消え、現われ、消えるのを見守った。自分が感じている虚無が、冷たい波となって打ち寄せてくるのをただ受けとめていた。

でもいまは、面接に呼ばれたのだ。「スティッチーズ」は自称、「クラシックなセンスを持った革新的なストア」であり、ヴィンテージのセーターを専門にしている。これでやっと、あの子供たちの死体以外を考えることができる——首筋で切断され、どろどろの、脈打つ、ピューッと噴き出す血に包まれて湿ってゆく死体以外のことを。代わりに彼は、何を着ていったらいいかを考えた。

なんとなく連帯感を表明しようと、以前キャンプに着ていっただぶだぶのカーゴパンツにイマニュエルは足をつっ込んだ。それから、エナメル革のス

---

❾ self-described as ...: 〜を自称している

❿ (an) innovator: 革新者

⓫ sever(ed): 〜を切断する

⓬ thick, pulsing, shooting blood: ドロドロで、脈打っている、噴き出している血

⓭ (a) move of solidarity: 連帯のしぐさ、表明

⓮ climb(ed) into ...: 〜に足をつっ込む。climb はこのように、服を着るしぐさにもよく使う。

⓯ cargoes: カーゴパンツ

stepped into his patent-leather ❶Space Jams ❷with the laces still clean and taut ❸as they weaved up all across the black tongue. Next, he pulled out a ❹long-ago abandoned black ❺hoodie and ❻dove into its tunnel. As a final act of solidarity, Emmanuel put

5 on ❼a gray snapback cap, a hat similar to the ones two of the Finkelstein Five had been wearing the day they were murdered—a fact George Wilson Dunn's ❽defense had stressed ❾throughout the proceedings.

Emmanuel stepped outside into the world, his Blackness at

10 a solid 7.6. He felt like ❿Evel Knievel at the top of a ramp. At the mall he'd look for something to wear to the interview, something to bring him down to at least a 4.2. He pulled ⓫the brim of his hat forward and down to ⓬shade his eyes. He walked up a hill toward Canfield Road, where he'd catch a bus. He ⓭listened to the gravel

15 scraping under his sneakers. It had been a very long time since he'd had his Blackness even close to a 7.0. "I want you safe. You gotta know ⓮how to move," his father had said to him at a very young age. Emmanuel started learning the basics of his Blackness

---

❶ Space Jams: スニーカーの定番。

❷ with the laces still clean and taut: 靴紐がいまだきれいでぴんと張っている

❸ as they weaved up all across the black tongue: 靴紐がジグザグにのびている姿を言っている。tongue は靴の「ベロ」。

❹ long-ago abandoned: ずっと前に見捨てた

❺ hoodie: パーカ

❻ dove into its tunnel: 直訳は「そのトンネルの中に飛びこんだ」。パーカを着る感覚を考えればそれほど奇抜ではない表現。dove は dive の過去。

❼ a ... snapback cap: うしろのスナップで大きさを調整できるようになっている野球帽。

ペースジャムを履く——靴紐はまだ綺麗でぴんとしていて、黒いベロの上をジグザグにのびている。次に、ずっと前にうっちゃった黒のフーディを引っぱり出し、そのトンネルに首をさし入れた。連帯の最後のしぐさとして、グレーのスナップバックキャップをかぶった。フィンケルスティーン・ファイブのうち二人が、殺された日にかぶっていたのと似た帽子である。ジョージ・ウィルソン・ダンの弁護団は、その帽子のことを裁判のあいだずっと強調していた。

　イマニュエルは世界へと歩み出た。黒人度はしっかり 7.6。ジャンプ台のてっぺんにいるイーヴル・クニーヴル、あの有名なスタントマンみたいな気分だった。モールへ行って、何かインタビューに着ていける服を探そう。最低 4.2 まで下げられるようなやつを。帽子のつばを前に引き下ろして、目の上にひさしが出来るようにした。坂道をキャンフィールド・ロードの方へ歩いていく。キャンフィールドでバスに乗るのだ。スニーカーの下で砂利がザクザクと鳴るのを聴いた。もうずいぶん長いこと、7.0 近くまで上がることさえなかったのに。「お前が安全でいてほしいんだ。お前は体の動かし方を学ばなくちゃいけない」と父親は、彼がまだひどく幼いときに言った。イマニュエルは割り算を覚えるよりも早く黒人度の基本を学んだ。腹が立ったら

❽ defense: 被告側（被告とその弁護士）
❾ throughout the proceedings: 裁判のあいだずっと
❿ Evel Knievel at the top of a ramp: ジャンプ台のてっぺんにいるイーヴル・クニーヴル。クニーヴルは実在した著名スタントマン（1938-2007）。
⓫ the brim of his hat: 帽子のつば
⓬ shade: 〜を影で覆う
⓭ listened to the gravel scraping: 砂利がザクザク鳴るのに耳を傾けた
⓮ how to move: どう動くか、どうふるまうか

before he knew how to do ❶long division: smiling when angry, whispering when he wanted to yell. ❷Back when he was in middle school, after a trip to the zoo, where he'd been accused of stealing ❸a stuffed panda from the gift shop, Emmanuel had burned ❹his last
5 pair of baggy jeans in his ❺driveway. He'd watched the denim ❻curl and ash in front of him ❼with unblinking eyes. When his father came outside, Emmanuel imagined he'd get a good ❽talking-to. Instead, his father stood quietly beside him. "This is an important thing to learn," his father had said. Together they watched the fire
10 until ❾it ate itself dead.

It was crowded at the bus stop. He felt eyes ❿shifting toward him while ⓫pocketbooks shifted away. Emmanuel thought of George Wilson Dunn. He imagined the middle-aged man standing there in front of him, smiling, a chain saw ⓬growling in his hands.
15 He decided to try something dangerous: he turned his hat backward so the shadow of the brim ⓭draped his neck. He felt

---

❶ long division: 長除法。742 を 3 で割るとき、まず 7 を 3 で割り、次にその余りと 4 を 3 で割り……と順次やっていく（要するに、普通の）割り算のこと。
❷ Back when ...: When ...と基本的に意味は変わらないが、ちょっと前のことをふり返っている感じが強まる。
❸ a stuffed panda: パンダのぬいぐるみ
❹ his ... pair of baggy jeans: 万引きしそうな子供、というレッテルを貼られそうなファッション、ということか。
❺ driveway: 表の道路から家・車庫までの私道。
❻ curl and ash: 丸まって灰になる。ash はこの場合自動詞。
❼ with unblinking eyes: まばたきもせず

ニコニコ笑い、わめきたくなったら小声でささやく。中学生のころ、遠足に行って、ギフトショップでパンダのぬいぐるみを盗んだと責められたとき、帰ってくるとイマニュエルは家の車庫の前で最後の一本のバギージーンズを燃やした。目の前でデニムが丸まり、灰になるのを彼はまばたきもせずに見守った。父親が外に出てくると、こっぴどく叱られるかと思ったが、父は彼と並んで黙って立っただけだった。「これはぜひ学ばなくちゃいけないことなんだ」と父は言った。火が燃えつきてひとりでに消えるまで二人は一緒に見守っていた。

　バス停は混んでいた。目がそっと彼の方に向けられ、ハンドバッグがそっと離れるのをイマニュエルは感じた。ジョージ・ウィルソン・ダンのことを彼は考えた。その中年男が自分の前に立ってニコニコ笑い、手に持ったチェーンソーがブンブン鳴っているところをイマニュエルは想像した。何か危険なことを試してみよう、と彼は決めた。帽子を前後ろにして、つばの影が首を覆うようにした。黒人度が8.0に跳ね上がり、針がぴくぴく震えるのを感じた。

❽ talking-to: お目玉。a good talking-to という形で使うことが多い。
❾ it ate itself dead: 燃え尽きて自然に消えた
❿ shift(ing): 動く
⓫ pocketbook(s): ハンドバッグ
⓬ growl(ing): うなる
⓭ drape(d): 〜を覆う

his Blackness ❶leap and throb to an 8.0. The people grew quiet.
They tried to look ❷superfriendly but also ❸distant, as if he were a
tiger or an elephant they were watching beneath a big tent. A path
through ❹the mass opened up for Emmanuel.

5   Soon, he was standing near the bench. A young woman with
long brown hair and a guy wearing sunglasses above the brim
of his hat both ❺remembered they had to be somewhere else,
immediately. An older woman remained sitting, and Emmanuel
took the newly available seat beside her. The woman glanced
10 toward Emmanuel as he sat. She smiled faintly. ❻Her look of
general disinterest ❼made his heart sing. He turned his hat
forward and felt his Blackness ease back to a ❽still very serious 7.6.
A minute later, the brown-haired woman returned and sat beside
him. She smiled like someone had told her that if she stopped
15 smiling ❾her frantic, wide-eyed smile Emmanuel would ❿blow her
brains out.

"The fact is, George Wilson Dunn is an American. Americans have

---

❶ leap and throb: 跳ね上がって、ぴくぴく疼く
❷ superfriendly: ものすごく友好的な
❸ distant: よそよそしい
❹ the mass: 人の群れ
❺ remembered they had to be somewhere else: いかにも「あっそうだ用を
　思い出した」という様子で立ち去ったということ。
❻ Her look of general disinterest: 概して何ごとにも興味のなさそうな顔
❼ made his heart sing: 直訳は「彼の心を歌わせた」。かすかに微笑んであとは
　無関心、というアメリカではまったく普通のふるまいをされて、イマニュエル
　がすごく嬉しくなることの悲哀。

人々が静かになった。みんなものすごく友好的な感じに、けれどよそよそしくも見えるよう努めている――あたかも彼が虎か象で、みんな大きなテントの下で見物しているかのように。イマニュエルが通れるよう道がさっと開いた。

じきに彼はバス停のベンチのそばに立っていた。長い茶色の髪の若い女と、帽子のつばの上にサングラスを載せた男が、二人とも即座に、どこか別の場所に用事があることを思い出した。年配の女性が一人、座ったままでいて、イマニュエルはその隣の空いたばかりの席に腰かけた。彼が座ると女性はイマニュエルの方をちらっと見た。そしてかすかにほほ笑んだ。何事にも興味のなさげなその様子に、イマニュエルの心が軽くなった。彼は帽子を前に押し戻し、黒人度が7.6まで下がるのを感じた。それでもまだ危うい数字だ。一分もすると、茶色い髪の女が戻ってきて彼の隣に座った。女はニコニコ笑っていた。もしその必死の、目を見開いたニコニコ笑いを一瞬でもやめたらそいつに脳味噌ブチ抜かれるぜ、と誰かに言われたみたいに笑いまくっていた。

「事実はですね、ジョージ・ウィルソン・ダンはアメリカ人だということです。アメリカ人には自分を護る権利があるんです」と弁護人は歌うような、チャー

❽ still very serious: まだ十分深刻な
❾ her frantic, wide-eyed smile: 必死そうな、目を見開いた笑顔
❿ blow her brains out: ピストルで脳味噌を吹っ飛ばす

the right to protect themselves," ❶the defense attorney says in a singing, charming voice. "Do you have children? Do you have anyone you love? ❷The prosecution has tried to ❸beat you over the head with scary words like 'law' and 'murder' and '❹sociopath.'"

5　The defense attorney's ❺index and middle fingers ❻claw the air repeatedly to indicate quotations. "I'm here to tell you that this case isn't about any of those things. It's about an American man's right to love and protect his own life and the life of his beautiful baby girl and his handsome young son. So I ask you, what do you

10　love more, the ❼supposed 'law' or your children?"

"❽I object?," says the ❾prosecuting attorney.

"❿I'll allow it, overruled," replies the judge as she ⓫dabs the now wet corners of her eyes. "Please continue, ⓬counselor."

"Thank you, ⓭Your Honor. I don't know about you all, but I

15　love my children more than I love the 'law.' And I love America more than I love my children. That's what this case is about:

❶ the defense attorney: 被告側の弁護士
❷ The prosecution: 検察側
❸ beat you over the head with ...: 〜をあなた方の頭に叩き込む
❹ sociopath: 社会病質者（人格に障害があり、反社会的な行動をとる人）
❺ index and middle fingers: 人差し指と中指
❻ claw the air repeatedly to indicate quotations: 引用符（quotations）を示すためにくり返し空気を引っかく（claw）。このフレーズは引用であって、「いわゆる」を付けて聞いてほしい、という意思表示に、アメリカではよく両手の二本指でこのしぐさをする。
❼ supposed: 仮定の、想像上の
❽ I object?: 異議あり？　文法的には疑問符は必要ない（むしろおかしい）が、語尾上がりの、ややこわばったか上ずったかしている口調を再現している。

ミングな声で言う。「皆さんには子供がいますか？　誰か愛する人がいますか？　検察側は『法律』『殺人』『社会病質者』といった怖い言葉を皆さんの頭に叩き込もうとしました」。弁護人の人差指と中指とが何度も空気を引っかいて引用符を作る。「いま私がここにいるのは、この裁判はそういう話ではないということを皆さんに伝えるためです。これは一人のアメリカ人男性が、自分自身の命を愛し、護り、可愛い幼い娘とハンサムな小さい息子の命を愛し、護るという話なのです。ゆえに私は皆さんにお訊ねします。皆さんはどちらをより愛するでしょうか、いわゆる『法律』をでしょうか、それとも自分の子供たちを？」

「異議あり？」と検察官が言う。

「異議を却下します」と女性裁判長は答え、潤んだ目元を拭う。「弁護人、続けてください」

「ありがとうございます、裁判長。皆さんのことはわかりませんが、私は『法律』を愛する以上に自分の子供たちを愛します。そして自分の子供たちを愛する以上にアメリカを私は愛します。この裁判はそういう話です。大文字の

❾ prosecuting attorney: 検察官
❿ I'll allow it, overruled: 弁護側の発言を許可し（allow）、検察の異議は却下された（overruled）ということ。
⓫ dab(s): 〜を軽く叩く、押さえる
⓬ (a) counselor: 法廷弁護士
⓭ Your Honor: 裁判官に対する敬称。

love with ❶a capital *L*. And America. That is what I'm defending here today. My ❷client, Mister George Dunn, believed he was in danger. ❸And you know what, if you believe something, anything, then that's what matters most. Believing. In America we have the
5 freedom to believe. America, our beautiful ❹sovereign state. Don't kill that here today."

The bus was ❺pulling in. Emmanuel noticed ❻a figure running toward the stop. It was Boogie, one of his best friends ❼from back
10 in grade school. In Ms. Fold's fourth-grade class, Emmanuel would ❽peek over at Boogie's tests during their history exams and then ❾angle his papers so Boogie could see his answers during ❿math tests. ⓫In all the years he'd known Boogie, ⓬he'd never known him to dress in anything but too-large T-shirts and baggy ⓭sweats.
15 By the time they were in high school, Emmanuel had learned to control his Blackness; Boogie had not. Emmanuel had ⓮quietly distanced himself from Boogie, who'd become known for fighting with other students and teachers. By now, he'd mostly forgotten

---

❶ a capital *L*: 大文字の L。たとえば "a Conservative with a capital C" といえば「根っからの保守主義者」(『リーダーズ英和辞典』)。

❷ (a) client: 依頼人

❸ And you know what: それでですね。you know what はこれから言うことに注意を促す言葉。

❹ sovereign state: 独立国家

❺ pull(ing) in: (乗り物が、止まるべき場所に) 入ってくる

❻ a figure: 人の姿

❼ from back in grade school: 小学校のころの

❽ peek over at ...: いかにも首をのばしてカンニングしている感じ。

Ｌのラブ、本物の愛の話なのです。そしてアメリカの話です。今日、私はそういうものを弁護しているのです。私の依頼人ミスター・ジョージ・ダンは、己の身が危険にさらされていると信じました。そして、いいですか皆さん、もし何かを、なんであれとにかく何かを信じるなら、それが何より大切なことになるのです。信じる。アメリカにおいて私たちは信じる自由を有しています。アメリカ、我らが美しき独立国家。今日ここでそれを殺さないでください。

　バスが停留所に近づいていった。ひとつの人影が停留所に向かって走ってくることにイマニュエルは気がついた。それは小学校のころの親友ブギーだった。ミズ・フォールドが担任の四年生のクラスで、イマニュエルは歴史のテストの最中ブギーの解答用紙を覗き込み、数学のテストになると自分の答案用紙を傾けてブギーに見えるようにしてやった。ブギーを知っていた年月、彼が大きすぎるＴシャツとだぶだぶのスウェットパンツ以外のものを着ているのを見たことは一度もなかった。二人とも高校に上がったころには、イマニュエルはもう黒人度を制御するすべを学んでいたがブギーは学んでいなかった。ほかの生徒たちや教師たちと年じゅう喧嘩することで有名なブギーから、イマニュエルはひっそり距離を置くようになった。もういまとなってはブギーのことをあらかた忘れてしまっていたが、たまに彼について

---

❾ angle:（ある角度に）～を曲げる
❿ math: mathematics（数学）
⓫ In all the years he'd known Boogie: ブギーと知り合いだった何年ものあいだ
⓬ he'd never known him to dress in anything but ...: 彼が～以外のものを着ているのを見たことがなかった
⓭ sweats: スウェットパンツ
⓮ quietly distanced himself from ...: ～から静かに距離を置いた

about him, but when Emmanuel did think of Boogie, it was with pity for him and ❶his static personhood. Boogie was always himself. Today, though, Boogie ran in black slacks, shining black dress shoes, a white button-up shirt, and a slim red tie. ❷His dress
5 combined with his sandy skin squeezed his Blackness down to a 2.9.

"❸Manny!" Boogie called as the bus pulled to a stop.

"❹What's good, bro," Emmanuel replied. In the past, Emmanuel had dialed his Blackness up whenever he was around
10 Boogie. Today he didn't have to. People ❺shuffled past them onto the bus. Emmanuel and Boogie ❻clapped palms and held the grip so that, with their hands between them, their chests came together, and when they took their hands back, ❼their fingers snapped against their palms.

15 Emmanuel said, "❽What you up to lately? What's new?"

"A lot, man. A lot. I've been waking up."

Emmanuel got on the bus, paid his $2.50, then found a seat near the back. Boogie took the empty seat beside him.

---

❶ his static personhood: 変化しない個性。ブギーは状況に合わせて Blackness を調節する、といったような細工とは無縁である。

❷ His dress combined with his sandy skin: その服が、砂色の肌と相まって

❸ Manny: Emmanuel の愛称。

❹ What's good, bro: よう、元気か。bro は brother。相手が元気かどうか真剣に訊ねているわけではないので疑問符はない。

❺ shuffled past them: ぞろぞろと横をすり抜けていった。トラブルを避けようと大人しく歩いている感じ。

❻ clapped palms: 手のひらをパンと合わせた

考えると、そのたびにブギーを憐れみ、いっこうに融通の利かない性格を憐れんだ。ブギーはつねに自分自身だったのだ。でも今日走っているブギーは黒いスラックスをはき、ピカピカの黒のドレスシューズ、白いボタンアップシャツ、赤いナロータイという格好だった。その服装に、砂っぽい薄茶色の肌とが相まって、黒人度は 2.9 にまで抑えられていた。

「マニー！」バスが停まると同時にブギーは叫んだ。

「よう、ブギー」とイマニュエルは答えた。過去にはブギーと一緒になるたび黒人度の目盛りを上げたものだった。今日はその必要もない。人々はぞろぞろと彼らの前を過ぎてバスに乗り込んでいった。イマニュエルとブギーはぱんと手のひらを合わせてぎゅっと握りあい、手を合わせたまま胸をくっつけ、手を元に戻すとき、たがいの手のひらで指をぱちんと鳴らした。

イマニュエルが「よう、最近どうしてる？　なんか変わったことあった？」と訊いた。

「いっぱい変わったよ。いっぱい。俺ね、目が覚めたんだ」

イマニュエルはバスに乗り込み、2 ドル 50 払い、奥の方に席をとった。ブギーもその隣の空いた席に座った。

---

❼ their fingers snapped against their palms: 指が相手の手のひらでぱちんと鳴った

❽ What you up to lately?: What are you up to lately?（最近どうしてる？）
up to …: 〜に携わって。非常によく使う。

"Yeah?"

"❶Yeah, man. I've been working lately. I'm trying to ❷get a lot of us together, man. We need to ❸unify."

"❹Word," Emmanuel replied ❺absently.

5 "I'm serious, bro. We need to move together. ❻We got to now. ❼You've seen it. You know ❽they don't give a fuck 'bout us now. They showed it." Emmanuel nodded. "We all need to unify. We need to ❾wake the fuck up. ❿I've been Naming. I'm getting a team together. ⓫You trying to ride or what?"

10 Emmanuel ⓬scanned the area around him ⓭to make sure no one had heard. It didn't seem like anyone had, but still he ⓮regretted his proximity to Boogie. "⓯You're not really doing that Naming stuff?" Emmanuel watched the smile on Boogie's face melt. Emmanuel ⓰made sure his face didn't do anything at all.

15 "Of course I am." Boogie unbuttoned the left cuff of his shirt and pulled the sleeve up. Along Boogie's inner ⓱forearm were three different marks. Each of them was a ⓲very distinct 5 ⓳carved

❶ Yeah, man: そうともさ。man はごく普通の呼びかけ。

❷ get a lot of us together: 俺たちを（仲間を）大勢集める

❸ unify: 一つになる

❹ Word: うん、そうだよな

❺ absently: ぼんやりした口調で

❻ We got to: We've got to = we have to

❼ You've seen it: フィンケルスティーン・ファイブの判決のことを言っている。

❽ they don't give a fuck 'bout us: 俺たちのことなんかどうでもいいと思ってる。'bout: about

❾ wake the fuck up: wake up を強めた表現。

❿ I've been Naming: ここで初めて出てくる Naming とは何なのか、この時点ではわからなくて当然。

「そうなのか？」

「そうなんだよ。俺、最近活動してんだ。大勢集めてるんだよ。俺たち、団結しないと」

「ああ」とイマニュエルは上の空で答えた。

「俺、本気だよ。俺たち一緒に動かないと。いまやらなくちゃ。お前も見ただろ。奴ら、俺たちのことなんかどうでもいいと思ってるんだ。あれではっきりしたよ」。イマニュエルも頷いた。「俺たちみんな団結しなくちゃ。目を覚まさなきゃいけないんだよ。俺な、ネーミングやってるんだよ。チーム作ってるんだ。どうだ、お前も乗るか？」

　イマニュエルは周りを見渡して誰にも聞かれていないことを確かめた。聞いた人間はいないみたいだったが、それでもブギーのそばにいることをイマニュエルは悔やんだ。「まさかお前、ほんとにあのネーミング、やってるのか？」。ブギーの顔の笑みが溶けてなくなるのをイマニュエルは見守った。自分の顔が何も変わらないようイマニュエルは気を張った。

「もちろんやってるさ」。ブギーはシャツの左のカフスを外して袖をまくり上げた。腕の内側に、三つ別々の印がついていた。それぞれ非常にはっきり

⓫ You trying to ride or what?: お前も乗るか、どうなんだ？

⓬ scan(ned): 〜をざっと見わたす

⓭ to make sure ...: 〜を確かめようと

⓮ regretted his proximity to Boogie: ブギーのそばにいることを悔やんだ。proximity:（距離や時間が）近いこと

⓯ You're not really doing that Naming stuff?: まさかお前、本当にあのネーミングってやつ（stuff）やってるんじゃないよな？　ネーミングが世の中ですでに話題になっているということがここでわかる。

⓰ made sure ...: 〜するよう気をつけた。註⓭と同じ。

⓱ forearm: 前腕。肘から手首までを言う。

⓲ very distinct: 非常にくっきりした

⓳ carved and scarred into his skin: 皮膚に彫られ、傷になって食い込んで

and scarred into his skin. After it was clear Emmanuel had seen, Boogie smoothed his sleeve back down over his arm but did not button the cuff. He continued in a low voice. "You know what my uncle said to me the other day?"

5   Emmanuel waited.

"He said that when you're on the bus and a tired man is ❶kinda leaning over beside you, using your shoulder like a pillow, people tell you to wake him up. They'll try to ❷sell it to you that the man needs to wake up and find some other place to rest ❸'cause ❹you
10 ain't a goddamn mattress."

Emmanuel made a sound to show he was following.

"But if he's sleeping ❺on his own, not ❻bothering you, it's supposed to be different. And if that sleeping man ❼gets ran up on by somebody that wants to ❽take advantage of him 'cause
15 he's asleep, 'cause he's so tired, everybody tries to tell you❾we're supposed to be, like, 'That's not my problem, ❿that don't got a thing to do with me,' as he ⓫gets his pockets all the way ran through or worse. ⓬

---

❶ kinda = kind of: なんとなく、ちょっと

❷ sell it to you that ...: 〜だとお前に信じさせる、思い込ませる

❸ 'cause: because

❹ you ain't a goddamn mattress: お前はマットレスなんかじゃねえんだ。ain't は aren't の崩れた言い方、goddamn は強調。

❺ on his own: 一人で（隣の人間に寄りかかったりせず）

❻ bother(ing): 〜に迷惑をかける

❼ gets ran up on by somebody: 誰かに寄ってこられ（て金などを奪われる）。「正しい」英語であれば ran は run（まあ正しい英語を話す人はそもそもこういう表現を使わないが）。

❽ take advantage of ...: 〜の弱みにつけ込む

と5が彫られ、肌に食い込んでいた。イマニュエルがちゃんと見たのを確かめてから、ブギーは袖を元に戻したがカフスのボタンは留めなかった。そして低い声で続けた。「俺の叔父がさ、こないだ何て言ったかわかるか？」

イマニュエルは待った。

「こう言ったんだよ。お前がバスに乗ってて、疲れた男が寄っかかってきて、お前を枕みたいに使ったら、そいつを起こせってみんなはお前に言う。そいつは起きなくちゃいけない、起きてどっかよそで休む場所を探さなきゃいけない、お前はマットレスじゃないんだからって」

聞いていることを示す音をイマニュエルは立てた。

「だけどもしそいつが一人で寝てて、お前の邪魔とかもしてなかったら、話は違うってことになってる。で、もし誰かが、そいつが疲れて眠ってるのにつけ込んで物とか盗んだりしても、みんなお前に言うんだよ、こういうときは『俺は関係ない、俺には全然関係ない』って考えるんだって、そいつがもうポケット空にされかけてたり、もっとひどい目に遭ってたりしても。

❾ we're supposed to be, like ...: 俺たちは、なんかこう、〜することになってる

❿ that don't got a thing to do with me: that has nothing to do with me

⓫ gets his pockets all the way ran through: ポケットの中身まるごと取られちまう。ran は註❼に同じ。

⓬ 段落の終わりでクォーテーションマークが閉じていないのは間違いではない。一人が複数の段落にわたって喋る場合、各段落のはじめに " が入り、最後の、喋り終わった段落の終わりにのみ " が入る。

"That man sleeping on the bus, he's your brother. That's what my uncle's saying. You need to protect him. Yeah, you might need to wake him up, but while he's asleep, he's your responsibility. Your brother, ❶even if you ain't met him a day in your life, ❷is your
5 business. ❸Feel me?"

Emmanuel ❹made another confirmatory sound.

Two days after the ruling, the first report had come through. An elderly white couple, both in their sixties, had had their brains
10 smashed in by a group armed with ❺bricks and rusty metal pipes. ❻Witnesses said the murderers had been dressed in ❼very fancy clothes: ❽bow ties and summer hats, cuff links and high heels. Throughout the double murder, ❾the group/gang had chanted, "Mboya! Mboya! Tyler Kenneth Mboya," the name of the eldest
15 boy killed at Finkelstein. The next day a similar story ❿broke. Three white schoolgirls had been killed with ice picks. A black man and black woman had poked holes through the girls' skulls ⓫like they were mining for diamonds. They ⓬chanted "Akua

---

❶ even if you ain't met him a day in your life: even if you have never met him in your life
❷ is your business: お前の務めなんだ、お前が責任負ってるんだ
❸ Feel me?: わかるか？
❹ made another confirmatory sound: 聞いてるよ、と伝える音をもう一度立てた
❺ bricks and rusty metal pipes: 煉瓦や錆びた金属パイプ
❻ Witness(es): 目撃者
❼ very fancy clothes: すごくお洒落な服
❽ bow tie(s): 蝶ネクタイ

　だけどな、バスでそうやって寝てる奴、そいつはお前のブラザーなんだよ。そう俺の叔父貴は言ってるわけだよ。お前はそいつを護ってやらなくちゃいけない。そう、起こしてやるべきかもしれない、だけどまだ寝てるあいだは、そいつはお前の責任なんだ。たとえいままで一度も会ったことなくたって、お前のブラザーなんだ、お前の仕事なんだよ。わかるか？」

　イマニュエルはふたたび確認の音を出した。

　判決の二日後、最初のニュースが伝わってきた。年配の、二人とも60代の白人カップルが、煉瓦と錆びた鉄パイプで武装したグループに脳を叩き潰された。目撃者によれば、殺人者たちはひどくお洒落な服装をしていたという。蝶ネクタイ、サマーハット、カフリンクス、ハイヒール。二人を殺害しているあいだずっと、グループ／ギャングは「ムボイヤ！　ムボイヤ！　タイラー・ケネス・ムボイヤ！」と、フィンケルスティーンで殺された最年長の男の子の名を唱えていたという。翌日同じような話が報じられた。三人の白人女子生徒がアイスピックで殺された。黒人の男女二人組が、女の子たちの頭蓋に、ダイヤモンドを掘り出そうとするみたいに穴を開けた。彼らは「ア

❾ the group/gang: 普通に言えばグループだが、凶暴さを重視すれば gang の方が相応しい。

❿ broke <break: 報道される

⓫ like they were mining for diamonds: as if they were mining … （ダイヤモンドでも採掘しているみたいに）

⓬ chant(ed): （単調な調子で）〜と唱える

Harris, Akua Harris, Akua Harris" all through the murder, according to reports. Again, the killers had been described as "quite fashionable, ❶given the circumstances." In both cases, the killers had been caught ❷immediately following the act. The couple that
5 killed the schoolgirls had carved the number 5 into their own skins just before the attack.

Several more cases of beatings and killings followed the first two. Each time the ❸culprits screamed the name of one of the Finkelstein Five. The Namers became ❹the latest terrorists on the
10 news. Most of the ❺perpetrators were killed by police officers before they could ❻be brought in for questioning. Those who were ❼detained spoke only the name of the child they'd used as a ❽mantra to their violence. None seemed interested in defense.

By far, the most famous of the Namers was Mary "Mistress"
15 Redding. The story was, Mistress Redding had been detained wearing a single ❾bloodstained white silk glove over her left hand, ❿once-sparkling white shoes with four-inch heels, and ⓫an A-line dress that was such ⓬a hard, rusty red that officers

---

❶ given the circumstances: 状況を考えれば、状況の割には。殺人という状況に、ファッショナブルな服装は普通結びつかない。
❷ immediately following the act: 犯行直後に
❸ culprit(s): 犯人
❹ the latest terrorists on the news: ニュースを賑わす最新のテロリストたち
❺ perpetrator(s): 加害者、犯人
❻ be brought in for questioning: 尋問のために（警察署に）連行される
❼ detain(ed): 〜を拘留する
❽ mantra: マントラ、呪文
❾ bloodstained: 血痕のついた

クア・ハリス、アクア・ハリス、アクア・ハリス」と殺害のあいだずっと唱えていたと報じられた。今回も、殺人者たちは「大変ファッショナブルな、けっこう場違いの」服装をしていたという。どちらの事件でも、殺人犯たちは犯行直後に捕まった。女子生徒たちを殺したカップルは、襲撃の直前に自分の肌に数字の5を彫っていた。

　殴打と殺害の事件が、この二つのあとさらにいくつか続いた。毎回犯人は、フィンケルスティーン・ファイブの一人の名を絶叫した。ネーマーたちはニュースでの最新テロリストとなった。犯人の大半は、尋問のために連行される間もなく警官に射殺された。拘留された者たちは、自分がふるまった暴力のマントラに使った子供の名前を口にするだけだった。誰一人、自分の身を護る気はないようだった。

　ネーマーたちのなかで図抜けて有名なのは、メアリ・「ミストレス」・レディングだった。話によると、ミストレス・レディングは、拘留されたとき左手に血のしみがついた白い絹の手袋をはめていて、10センチのヒール付きのかつてはピカピカだった白い靴をはき、Aラインのワンピースを着ていた。ワンピースのあざやかな、錆色っぽい赤を見て、それがもとは真っ白だった

❿ once-sparkling white: 元はきらきら光る白さだった
⓫ an A-line dress: Aラインのワンピース。上がぴったり締まって、下の方はゆるやかに広がっている。
⓬ a hard, rusty red: あざやかな、錆のような赤

couldn't believe it had originally been a perfect white. For hours, Redding answered all of the questions with a single name. *Why did you do it?* "J. D. Heroy." *He was just a child!* ❶*How could you?* "J. D. Heroy." *Who are you working with? Who is your leader?* "J.
5 D. Heroy." *Do you feel any* ❷*remorse for what you've done?* "J. D. Heroy." *What is it* ❸*you people want?* "J. D. Heroy." Redding had been caught with a group that had killed a single teenage boy, but there was ❹a train of ten 5s carved into her back that ❺trailed down to her left thigh, including one that was ❻dripping and fresh
10 when she was caught. According to reports, several hours into ❼an advanced interrogation session, a single sentence had ❽escaped Mistress Redding. "If I had words left in me, I would not be here."

Emmanuel remembered how the news had reported ❾the bloody phenomenon: "❿Breaking this evening," said one anchor,
15 "⓫yet another innocent child was ⓬mercilessly beaten by a gang of ⓭thugs, all of whom seem, again, to be ⓮descendants of the African diaspora. What do you think of this, Holly?"

---

❶ *How could you?*: How could you do it, How could you do such a terrible thing?
❷ remorse: 良心の呵責、後悔の念
❸ you people: お前ら
❹ a train of ...: ひと連なりの〜
❺ trail(ed) down to ...: 下っていって〜に行きつく
❻ dripping and fresh: まだ血が滴り、「出来立て」で
❼ an advanced interrogation session: 直訳は「より進んだ尋問の場」。
❽ escape(d):（言葉などが）思わず漏れ出る
❾ the bloody phenomenon: その血なまぐさい事件
❿ Breaking this evening: 今夜の速報です

とは警官たちには信じられなかった。何時間もずっと、レディングはすべての質問にひとつの名前で答えた。なぜやったんだ？「J・D・ヘロイ」。まだ子供だったんだぞ！　どうしてあんなひどいことを？「J・D・ヘロイ」。誰と活動しているのか？　リーダーは誰か？「J・D・ヘロイ」。やったことを後悔しているか？「J・D・ヘロイ」。お前たちは何が望みなのか？「J・D・ヘロイ」。一人のティーンエージャーの少年を殺したグループとともにレディングは捕まったが、彼女の背中には数字の5が10個連なって彫られ、左の太腿まで下りていて、うちひとつは捕まったときまだ乾いておらず血が滴っていた。報道によれば、より厳しい尋問が何時間か続いた時点で、ミストレス・レディングの口からひとつのセンテンスが漏れたという。「あたしのなかに言葉が残ってたら、こんなところにいやしない」

　流血の事態をニュースがどう報じたかをイマニュエルは思い起こした。「今夜ふたたび」とあるキャスターは言った。「またも罪のない子供が暴漢の一団によって無慈悲に撲殺されました。今回もまた、一団の全員がアフリカからの離散民の子孫であるようです。ホリー、これをどう考えたらいいのだろう？」

❶ yet another ...: さらにまた一人の〜
⓬ mercilessly: 無慈悲に、冷酷に
⓭ thug(s): 暴漢
⓮ descendants of the African diaspora: アフリカ離散の民の子孫たち。「黒人」を思いきり遠回しに言っている。

177

"Well, many people in the streets are saying, and ❶I quote, 'I told you they don't know how to act! We told you.' ❷Beyond that, all I can say is this violence is terrible." The ❸coanchor shook her head, ❹disgusted.

5   The names of each of the Finkelstein Five had become ❺curses. When no one was around, Emmanuel liked to say the names to himself: Tyler Mboya, Fela St. John, Akua Harris, Marcus Harris, J. D. Heroy.

10 "This is just the beginning," Boogie said. He pulled a small ❻box cutter out of his pocket. Emmanuel almost made a sound, but Boogie said, "Don't worry, I'm not ❼gonna use it. Not here. I ❽haven't gone all the way—yet." Emmanuel watched Boogie as he rolled up his sleeve for the second time and, ❾with a practiced
15 precision, used five quick slashes to cut a small 5 into his left arm. The skin split into ❿a thin red that gathered, then rolled down the side of his arm.

Boogie reached over Emmanuel and pulled the yellow cord.

---

❶ I quote: 「ここからは他人の言葉の引用です」ということを示す言い方。
❷ Beyond that: それ以上は
❸ coanchor: キャスター仲間
❹ disgusted: うんざりして
❺ curse(s): 呪いの言葉
❻ (a) box cutter: カッターナイフ
❼ gonna: going to
❽ haven't gone all the way — yet: とことんやってはいない——まだ。殺人は まだ犯していないということ。
❾ with a practiced precision: 慣れた様子の正確さで

「そうですねえ、まあ街で多くの人が言っているのは、『言っただろう、奴らはどうふるまったらいいかわからないんだ！ 私たちが言ったとおりだよ』といったたぐいのことですね。これ以上はもう、とにかく恐ろしい暴力だ、としか言えませんね」。そして女性キャスターは嫌悪の念もあらわに首を横に振った。

フィンケルスティーン・ファイブそれぞれの名前がいまや呪いの言葉と化した。周りに誰もいないとき、イマニュエルはそれらの名前を好んで呟いた。タイラー・ムボイヤ、フェラ・セントジョン、アクア・ハリス、マーカス・ハリス、J・D・ヘロイ。

「これはまだほんの始まりだ」とブギーは言った。そして小さなカッターナイフをポケットから出した。イマニュエルは思わず音を立てかけたが、ブギーは「心配するな。使いやしないから。ここでは。まだとことんやっちゃいないんだ——いまのところは」と言った。イマニュエルが見守るなか、ブギーはもう一度袖をまくり、いかにも慣れた手つきで、ささっとすばやく小さな5を左腕に切り込んだ。肌が裂けて細い赤が現われ、赤がだんだん集まってきて、やがて腕の側面を流れ落ちていった。

ブギーがイマニュエルの向こう側に腕をのばして、黄色い紐を引っぱった。

---

❿ a thin red that gathered, then rolled down ...: 血の動きを描写している。

There was a ❶*bing* sound and the STOP REQUESTED sign went bright. The bus slowed in front of Market Plaza.

"I'm gonna ❷hit you up later, Manny. We're going to need you."

5 "❸Got it. ❹I have the same number," Emmanuel said as the bus stopped.

Boogie walked to the bus's rear door. He turned, smiled at Emmanuel, then ❺at the top of his lungs screamed, "J. D. HEROY!" The name was still echoing off the windows when Boogie took
10 his ❻fist and ❼crashed it against a white woman's jaw. She didn't make a sound. She ❽slumped over in her seat. Boogie pulled his fist back again and punched the woman in the face a second time. A third. It sounded like hammering a nail into soft wood.

"Help!" somebody sitting near the woman screamed. "❾Fuck
15 you, asshole," another yelled as Boogie jumped out the bus's back door and ❿sprinted away. No one followed him. Emmanuel pulled his cell phone out of his pocket and dialed ⓫911. As he called, he stepped toward the crowd that had formed around the woman.

---

❶ *bing*: ベルの音を表わす擬音語。
❷ hit you up later: そのうち連絡する
❸ Got it: わかった
❹ I have the same number: 電話番号は変わっていない、ということ。
❺ at the top of his lungs: 声を限りに
❻ (a) fist: 握りこぶし
❼ crash(ed): 叩きつける
❽ slumped over: どさっと倒れ込んだ
❾ Fuck you, asshole: くたばれ、クソ野郎
❿ sprinted away: 走り去った

ピンという音がして、**つぎ停まります**のランプが明るく灯った。マーケット・プラザの前でバスは速度を落とした。

「そのうち連絡するからな、マニー。いずれお前が必要になるからさ」

「わかった。番号、変わってないから」バスが停まるとともにイマニュエルは言った。

　ブギーはバスの後方ドアまで歩いていった。ふり返って、イマニュエルに向かってにっこり笑い、それからありったけの大声で「Ｊ・Ｄ・ヘロイ！」と叫んだ。その名がまだ窓から谺している最中に、ブギーはこぶしを作って、そこにいた白人女性のあごに叩きつけた。女性は何の音も立てなかった。座ったまま、力なく前に倒れた。ブギーはもう一度こぶしをうしろに引いて、もう一度女性の顔にパンチを浴びせた。三発目。柔らかい材木に釘を打ち込んでいるみたいだった。

「助けて！」女性のそばに座っていた誰かが悲鳴を上げた。「この野郎、何てことするんだ」と別の誰かが、バスの後方ドアから飛び降りて走り去っていくブギーに向かってどなった。誰も追っていかなかった。イマニュエルはポケットから携帯を出して911にかけた。電話しながら、女性の周りに群がった人たちの方に寄っていった。女性の鼻は折れて、血が流れていた。血がど

⓫ 911: 日本の110番と119番を合わせたような緊急電話番号。nine one one または nine eleven と読む。

Her nose was ❶busted and bleeding. The blood rolled out ❷in a steady leak and had bubbles in it. Again, Emmanuel felt a ticking and grinding in his chest. He ❸gritted his teeth and closed his eyes. ❹He imagined the color sky blue.

5　　"Hi. I'm on a bus and ❺this lady is hurt. Yeah, ❻we're on Myrtle, right by Market Plaza. Yeah, she's hurt pretty bad." He could feel fear ❼swelling toward him. He'd been next to Boogie and at 7.6. The bus sat on the roadside, and a small group of passengers made a wall around the woman. The other passengers ❽took
10　turns shooting ❾hard stares at Emmanuel. He imagined the police officers ❿blasting through the bus doors and the many fingers that would immediately point in his direction. He imagined the bullet that would not take even a second to find his brain. He'd never stolen a thing in his life; he ⓫didn't even particularly like pandas.
15　He got off the bus, ignoring the murmurs and trying hard not to look at the woman with the broken face. He walked a few blocks to a nearby bus stop.

*

❶ bust(ed): 〜を折る
❷ in a steady leak: 間断なく漏れ出て
❸ gritted his teeth: 歯を食いしばった
❹ He imagined the color sky blue: おそらくイマニュエルはここで必死に落ち着こうとしている。
❺ this lady is hurt: この this は、「いまからこのことについて話します」という意を伝える。また p. 86 の註❻を参照。
❻ we're on Myrtle: 居場所を伝えるために、まず通りの名を言っている。
❼ swelling toward him: 膨らんでこっちへやって来る
❽ took turns ... ing: 代わるがわる〜した

くどく流れ出て、泡が立っていた。ふたたび胸がカチッ、ギリギリと締めつけられるのをイマニュエルは感じた。歯を食いしばって、目を閉じた。青空の色を想像した。

「もしもし。いまバスに乗ってるんですけど、女性がケガしたんです。ええ、マートルにいます、マーケットプラザのすぐ前です。はい、けっこうひどい怪我です」。恐怖心が大きく膨らんで迫ってくるのが感じられた。さっきまでブギーといて、黒人度は7.6。バスは道端に駐まっていて、乗客たちの小集団が女性の周りに壁を作っていた。ほかの乗客たちは代わるがわるイマニュエルを睨みつけていた。警官たちが乗降ドアから飛び込んできて大勢の指がいっせいに彼の方を指す情景をイマニュエルは想像した。彼の脳にたどり着くのに一秒とかからない銃弾を想像した。生まれてこのかた、物を盗んだことは一度もない。パンダなんてべつに好きでもないのだ。ブツブツ呟く声を無視してイマニュエルはバスを降り、顔を破壊された女性の方を見ないよう精一杯自分を抑えた。何ブロックか歩いて、次のバス停まで行った。

*

❾ hard stares: 冷たいまなざし
❿ blast(ing) through ...: 〜から飛び込んでくる
⓫ didn't even particularly like pandas: パンダなんてとりわけ好きでもなかった（なのにぬいぐるみを盗んだと責められた）

The mall was as it always was. Parents ran from store to store; their children **❶**struggled to keep pace. Three **❷**security guards **❸**tailed Emmanuel from the moment he stepped into the mall. Whenever he slowed or stopped, the guards **❹**jumped into conversation or pretended to listen to important information via their **❺**two-way radios. Normally, when Emmanuel went to the mall, he wore blue jeans that weren't too baggy or tight and **❻**a nice collared shirt. He **❼**smiled ear to ear and walked very slowly, only **❽**eyeing any one thing in any store for a maximum of twelve seconds. Emmanuel's usual mall Blackness was **❾**a smooth 5.0. Usually only one security guard followed him.

He went into a store named Rodger's. He chose an **❿**eggshell blue button-up, then handed the shirt to a cashier. The cashier took his card and ran it through the machine. Then she folded his shirt and **⓫**tucked it into **⓬**a plastic bag.

"I need a receipt," Emmanuel said, then thanked her as she handed him the **⓭**flimsy white paper. He dropped it into the bag with his shirt. When he approached the store's entrance/exit, he

---

❶ struggled to keep pace: 必死に遅れまいとして
❷ security guard(s): 警備員
❸ tail(ed): 〜のあとをつける
❹ jumped into conversation: 急に会話を始めた
❺ two-way radios: ウォーキートーキー、トランシーバー
❻ a nice collared shirt: 襟もちゃんとあるきちんとしたシャツ
❼ smiled ear to ear: 満面の笑みを浮かべた
❽ eye(ing): 〜を見る
❾ a smooth 5.0: p. 156 で 7.6 は "solid" だったが、5.0 は "smooth"——「穏当な」というところか。

　モールはいつもと変わらなかった。親たちが店から店へと駆け回り、子供たちが懸命に追いかける。イマニュエルがモールに入った瞬間から、警備員が三人あとをつけてきた。彼が歩みを緩めたり、立ちどまったりするたび、警備員たちはいきなりお喋りを始めたり、ウォーキートーキーで重要な情報を聴いているふりをした。ふだんモールに行くときは、だぶだぶ過ぎずきつ過ぎもしないブルージーンズをはき、ちゃんと襟のついたシャツを着るようにしている。口が裂けそうな笑みを浮かべて、すごくゆっくり歩き、どの店のいかなる品も最大12秒以上は決して見ないように留意する。イマニュエルのふだんのモールでの黒人度は穏便な5.0だった。いつもは一人の警備員しかついて来なかった。

　ロジャーズという店に入った。エッグシェルブルーのボタンアップシャツを選び、レジに持っていった。レジ係が彼のカードを受けとって機械に通した。それからシャツを畳んでビニール袋に入れた。

「レシート下さい」とイマニュエルは言い、ぺらぺらの白い紙を受けとりながら係の女性に礼を言った。レシートを袋のなかに入れた。店の出入口に近づくと、手首を引っぱられるのを感じた。ふり向くと、店の名札をシャツに

---

⑩ eggshell blue: 薄い青緑
⑪ tuck(ed): 〜をしまい込む、入れる
⑫ a plastic bag: ビニール（ポリ）袋
⑬ flimsy: ペラペラの

❶felt a tug on his wrist. He turned to see a tall man with a store name tag pinned to his shirt.

"Did you purchase that shirt, sir?" The man's voice was ❷condescending and sharp, like a cruel teacher's or a villain's from
5 a children's television show. Immediately, Emmanuel felt habit ❸telling him to be precisely gentle, to smile, and not to yell ❹no matter what. He pushed habit away as he ❺snatched his hand back from the man.

"Yeah, actually I did," Emmanuel said in a voice loud enough
10 to make shoppers turn and stare.

"Do you have a receipt for that purchase that you actually made?"

"Yes, I do."

"Can I please see this receipt that you actually have for that
15 purchase you actually made?"

"Well, I can show it to you," Emmanuel began. "Or maybe ask the cashier who ❻rang me up two seconds ago." He ❼jabbed a finger in the direction of the register. He felt his Blackness

---

❶ felt a tug on his wrist: 手首が引っぱられるのを感じた
❷ condescending: 慇懃無礼な、見下したような
❸ telling him to be precisely gentle: ここはしっかり大人しくやれと告げて
❹ no matter what: 何があっても
❺ snatched his hand back: 手をさっと引いた。習慣が命じるのとは正反対の乱暴なしぐさ。
❻ rang me up: 俺が買った品をレジに打ち込んだ
❼ jabbed a finger: 指をぐいっと突き出した。これもふだんは避けているであろう乱暴なしぐさ。

留めた背の高い男だった。

「お客様、そのシャツはご購入になりましたか?」。小馬鹿にした、ギスギスした声で、残酷な教師か、子供向け番組の悪者を思わせた。ここはしっかり穏やかに、と習慣が即座にイマニュエルに命じた。ニッコリ笑って、何があっても声を荒げないように、と。イマニュエルは習慣を払いのけ、摑まれた手をさっとふりほどいた。

「ああ、ほんとに購入したよ」とイマニュエルは、周りの客が驚いてふり向くくらいの大声で言った。

「その、ほんとになさったご購入のレシートはお持ちですか?」

「ああ、持ってるよ」

「それではそのほんとになさったご購入を証明するほんとにお持ちのレシートを拝見できますか?」

「ああ、見せてもいいよ」とイマニュエルは言いかけた。「いやそれとも、二秒前にレジ打ってくれた係の人に訊いてもいいんじゃないかね」。彼はレ

❶creeping up toward 8.1. He was angry and alive and free. When the cashier looked up and saw what was happening, she raised a hand and ❷waved with her fingers.

"Hmm, so do you have a receipt or not?"

5　　Emmanuel stared at the man. Then he handed him the receipt. Emmanuel had had this conversation a number of times before. Not so much since he'd really learned to ❸lock down to sub-6.0 levels.

"❹Can't be too careful," the man said, and handed the receipt

10　back. Emmanuel ❺knew better than to wait for ❻an apology. He turned and left the store and felt himself slide back down to a 7.6 in the eyes of ❼the mallgoers around him.

As Emmanuel ❽made his way back to the bus stop, a different pair of security guards followed closely behind him, but far

15　enough away to make it seem like they were just ❾walking in the same direction he was. Emmanuel stopped to tie his shoe, and one of the security guards jumped behind ❿a decorative potted plant while the other stared off into the sky, whistling. They followed

---

❶ creep(ing) up: じわじわ上がる

❷ waved with her fingers: 指を振って合図した。その人ちゃんと買いましたよ、というしぐさだが、警備員はそれでも引かない。

❸ lock down to sub-6.0 levels: 6.0 以下のレベルにきっちり下がる

❹ Can't be too careful: 用心しすぎということはない

❺ knew better than to ...: ～するほど馬鹿ではなかった。know は「知識」ではなく「知恵」の問題。p. 60, l. 7 に既出。

❻ an apology: 謝罪

❼ the mallgoers: モールの客たち

❽ made his way back to ...: ～に戻っていった

ジの方を突き刺すように指を向けた。黒人度がじわじわ8.1まで上がるのを感じた。彼は怒っていて、生きていて、自由だった。レジ係が顔を上げて事態を呑み込むと、彼女は片手を上げて指を振ってみせた。

「ふむ、で、レシートはお持ちなんですか、お持ちでないんですか？」

イマニュエルは男をじっと見た。それから、男にレシートを渡した。こういう会話はもう何度もやったことがあった。6.0以下に落とすことをしっかり学んでからはそんなにやらなくなっていた。

「用心に越したことはないからね」と男は言ってレシートを返してきた。謝罪の言葉を待つほどイマニュエルはお目出度くなかった。男に背を向けて店を出た。周りのモール客たちから見て7.6まで落ちていくのが感じられた。

バス停まで戻っていく最中、別の警備員二人組がすぐうしろ、だが単にたまたま同じ方向に歩いているだけに思えるくらい離れてあとをつけて来た。イマニュエルが立ちどまって靴紐を結び直すと、一方の警備員はさっと観葉

❾ walking in the same direction he was: 彼と同じ方向に歩いている
❿ a decorative potted plant: 装飾用の鉢植え植物

him to the south exit bus stop, then turned back into the mall once he was seated beneath the **❶**overhang.

Emmanuel **❷**found a window seat. No one sat next to him. The bus had just started moving when his phone buzzed. He 5 recognized the number as the same one that had called him that morning. He pushed the green dot on the screen, immediately setting his voice to a 1.5.

"Hello. You've reached Emmanuel."

"Hey there, son, I called this morning about **❸**an interview we 10 thought about lining up for you." The man's voice was **❹**full and husky.

"Yes, I'm looking forward to it. Tomorrow at eleven, correct?"

"Well, the thing is and—**❺**I really hate to be this guy, but I just **❻**thought I might save you some time. **❼**It's Emmanuel Gyan, 15 right?"

"Yes, that's correct."

"Well, Emmanuel, **❽**thing is, and shit, I **❾**didn't think things all the way through, but **❿**I think we might have that position filled

---

❶ overhang: 張り出し

❷ found a window seat: こういう場合 find は「見つける」とは少し違う。それほど「探す」行為が伴っているわけではなく、単に「窓側の席が空いていたので座った」という程度。

❸ an interview we thought about lining up for you: 直訳は「あんたのために設定することを考えた面接」。

❹ full and husky: 太くてしゃがれた

❺ I really hate to be this guy: この男になるのは本当に嫌だ＝こんな役回りは嫌だ

❻ thought I might save you some time: 君に時間を無駄にさせなくていいようにしてやれるかと思って

植物の陰に隠れ、もう一方は空を見上げて口笛を吹いた。二人とも南出口の
バス停までつけて来て、イマニュエルが張出しの下のベンチに座るとモール
に戻っていった。

　イマニュエルは窓側の席に座った。誰も隣に座らなかった。バスが動き出
したところで携帯が振動した。番号を見てみると、けさかかってきたのと同
じだった。画面の緑色の点をタップし、即座に声を 1.5 に調整した。
「もしもし。こちらイマニュエルです」
「やあどうも。けさおたくの面接を決めたと思って電話した者です」。男の
声は太く、しゃがれていた。
「ええ、楽しみにしています。明日の 11 時でしたよね」
「うんいや、それがね——いや本当にこういうこと伝えるのは嫌な役回りな
んだが、無駄足運ばせても、と思ってねえ。あなたお名前、イマニュエル・
ジアンだよね？」
「はい、そうです」
「でね、イマニュエル、実はね、いやぁその、さっきはちゃんと考えてなく
てね、この求人、もう埋まっちゃってるかもしれないみたいでね」

---

❼ It's Emmanuel Gyan, right?:（あんたの名前）イマニュエル・ジアンだよね？
　Gyan はガーナ系に多い名。相手はイマニュエルが何系かを確かめている。

❽ thing is, and shit: つまりさ……いやーそれがね

❾ didn't think things all the way through: いろんなことをきちんと考えなかっ
　た

❿ I think we might have that position filled already: その口、もうすでに埋
　まっちゃっているかもしれないと思うんだ。何とももって回った言い方。

already."

"Pardon?"

"Well, thing is, we have this guy Jamaal here already, and then there's also Ty, who's half-Egyptian. So I mean, it'd be **❶**overkill.

5 **❷**We aren't an urban brand. You know what I mean? So I thought it'd—" Emmanuel ended the call and tried very hard to breathe. Again, his phone buzzed. He eyed the screen hard; it was a message from Boogie. *The park 10:45.*

10 "Mister Dunn." The defense attorney **❸**sashays to **❹**the bench. "What were you doing on **❺**the night in question before you encountered **❻**the five people you say attacked you?"

"Well." George Wilson Dunn looks at his attorney, then at the jury. "I was with my children at the library. Both of them. Tiffany

15 and Rodman. I'm a single father."

"A single father out with his children at the library. So what happened before you went outside?" The defense attorney looks curious, **❼**as if this were all news to him.

---

❶ overkill: やりすぎ

❷ We aren't an urban brand: うちは都会のブランドじゃないから（都会のブランドだったら、マイノリティを大勢雇っています、ということを大々的に打ち出すかもしれないが）

❸ sashay(s): 気取って歩く

❹ the bench: 裁判官席

❺ the night in question: 問題の夜

❻ the five people you say attacked you: 直訳は「あなたを襲ったとあなたが言う五人」

❼ as if this were all news to him: 初耳だというように

「は？」

「いやその、うちにはもうジャマアルっていうのがいてね、あとタイってのがいてこれが半分エジプト系で。だから、さらにもう一人ってのはちょっとやり過ぎだろうと。うちは都会派ブランドとかじゃないからね。わかるかな、言ってること。だからそれで──」イマニュエルは電話を切って、息をしようと精一杯努めた。また携帯が振動した。画面をまじまじと見た。ブギーからのメッセージだった。**公園、10:45。**

「ミスター・ダン」。弁護人は気取った足どりで裁判官席に向かう。「問題の夜、あなたを襲ったとおっしゃる五人に遭遇する前、あなたは何をなさっておられましたか？」

「そうですねえ」。ジョージ・ウィルソン・ダンは弁護士を見て、それから陪審員たちを見る。「子供と一緒に図書館にいました。子供たち二人ともです。ティファニーとロドマン。私、シングルファーザーなもんで」

「シングルファーザーが子供たちと出かけて図書館にいたと。で、外に出る前に何があったんでしょう？」。弁護人はあたかもこれが初めて聞く話だとでもいうように興味津々に見える。

"Thing is, being a father is the most important thing in the world to me. And being a father of two kids like Tiffany and Rodman, **❶**you just never know what you're going to get.

"That night, as we're looking around the movie section for
5 something to watch that weekend. Tiffany **❷**out and says she's not going to school anymore 'cause she's fat and ugly, and all of a sudden I've got this crisis on my hands. And she's the older one, usually gives me less trouble. **❸**But that's being a parent. No **❹**prep. She's never said anything like this before, and all of a sudden you
10 have to **❺**fix it or else she'll become **❻**some kinda bum or **❼**crack whore."

"This is **❽**irrelevant, Your Honor," the prosecuting attorney says from her chair.

"I'll allow it, but **❾**get on with your story, Mister Dunn."

15 "**❿**This *is* the story," Dunn says. "So **⓫**outta nowhere I gotta **⓬**figure out something to say to my only daughter to **⓭**put her back on track. And all the while, my only boy, he's quiet and not saying

---

❶ you just never know what you're going to get: 何を得るかまったくわか らない＝何が起きるかわかったものじゃない

❷ out and says: 出し抜けに言い出す。このように過去の話を現在形で語るのは 珍しくない（あまり知的には響かないが）。out and ...（いきなり〜する）は up and ... という形の方がより一般的。

❸ But that's being a parent: だがそれが親であることだ＝親をやってりゃよく あることだ

❹ prep: preparation（準備）

❺ fix: 〜を解決する

❻ some kinda bum: some kind of bum。(a) bum: 浮浪者

❼ (a) crack whore: クラック漬けの売春婦。クラックは安価で強いドラッグで、

「いやその、父親であるってことは私にとって世界で一番大事なことなわけ
ですよ。で、ティファニーとロドマンみたいな子供の父親だとですね、これ
はもう何があるかわからないわけですよ。

　あの夜、私たちは映画セクションにいて、週末に何を観ようかと物色して
ました。するとティファニーが出し抜けに、あたしもう学校行かない、あた
しデブでブスだからって、こっちはもういきなりピンチです。何しろあの子
はお姉ちゃんで、ふだんは弟より手がかからない。でもまあ親をやってれば
そんなもんです。前ぶれも何もありゃしません。あの子がそんなこと言った
こと、いままで一度もないんです、それが突然こっちは何とかしなくちゃい
けない、じゃなきゃあの子は浮浪者だか、ヤク中の娼婦だかになっちまう」
「これは無関係です、裁判長」と検察官席に座った女性が言う。
「続けてよろしい、ですが本筋に戻ってください、ミスター・ダン」
「いやいや、これが本筋なんです」とダンは言う。「でね、こっちはいきなり、
たった一人の娘に何か言って、元に戻してやらないといけない。そのあいだ
ずっと、たった一人の息子の方は、大人しくしていて、一言も喋らない。で、

　多くの人間の人生を破壊した。
❽ irrelevant: 無関係な
❾ get on with your story:（脇道にそれずに）話を進めなさい
❿ This *is* the story: これが話なんです（脇道なんかじゃありません）
⓫ outta nowhere: out of nowhere（いきなり）
⓬ figure out …: 〜を思いつく、考え出す。p. 130, l. 7 などに既出。
⓭ put her back on track: 正しい状態に戻してやる

a word this whole time, and that has me almost more worried than anything else. I love the kid, but ❶ he's a crazy one. So as we're getting ready to leave the library, I tell Tiffany how she's beautiful and how Daddy loves her and how that will never change. And
5 you know what she says? She says, 'Okay,' ❷ like it's all fixed. Like ❸ she just wanted me to say that one thing. And ❹ I can finally breathe. Then the other one, Rodman, pushes over a cart that ❺ crashes into a shelf and makes about a hundred DVDs ❻ crash down to the floor. But that's being a parent, ya know? Anyway,
10 that's what happened before I got outside."

"All right, and when you were outside?" the defense asks with a warm smile.

"When I got outside, I was attacked. And I protected myself and both my kids."

15 "And, on this night in question, were your actions motivated by the love you feel for your children and your ❼ God-given right to protect yourself and them?"

"They were."

---

❶ he's a crazy one: 無茶苦茶な子だ
❷ like it's all fixed: 万事解決という感じに。like は as if のくだけた言い方。
❸ she just wanted me to say that one thing: その一言だけ言ってほしかった
❹ I can finally breathe: これでやっとひと息つける
❺ crash(es) into a shelf: 棚に突っ込む
❻ crash down to the floor: ガラガラ音を立てて落ちる
❼ God-given: 神から与えられた、生得の

こっちの方が実はもっと心配なくらいで。可愛くて仕方ない子ですが、もう無茶苦茶なんです。それでそろそろ図書館を出ようってところで、ティファニーに言ってやったんです、お前はほんとにキレイだよ、パパお前のこと大好きだよ、それは絶対変わらないよって。そしたら何て言ったと思います？『わかった』って言ったんです。もう何もかも決まりって感じで。そのことだけ言ってほしかったんだって感じで。これで私もやっと一息つけました。そしたらもう一人が、ロドマンがね、カートを押したらそれが棚にぶつかっちゃって、DVDが100枚くらいガラガラガラって床に落ちて。でもまあ親をやってればそんなもんです。まあとにかく、外に出る前にあったのはそういうことで」

「わかりました、で、外に出たら？」弁護人は温かい笑みを浮かべて訊く。

「外に出たら、襲われたんです。で私は、自分と子供二人を護ったんです」

「それで、問題のこの夜、あなたの行動は、お子さんたちに対して感じる愛情と、神から与えられた自分と子供を護る権利に促されていたのでしょうか？」

「そうです」

"No further questions, Mister Dunn."

Emmanuel greeted his parents with a smile when they got home. They ate dinner together as a family, though Emmanuel hardly
5 spoke a word. After they were finished, Emmanuel's father told him he was proud of him no matter what happened at the interview and that he should wear a tie and try to speak slowly. "You'll do great," he said.

When his parents were asleep, Emmanuel slipped into the
10 shower. He got out, combed his hair, then put on ❶fresh underwear and socks. He pulled and zipped himself into ironed ❷tan slacks. He looped a brown leather belt around his waist. Then he put on a white undershirt and the eggshell blue button-up. He tied the laces of his wing-tipped dress shoes tightly.
15 Emmanuel moved slowly out of his room and out of the house. He closed the side door as quietly as he could manage and was in the garage. There was an aluminum bat leaning against ❸a wall with peeling paint. He stared at the bat. The grinding, clicking heat

❶ fresh: 新品の
❷ tan: タンカラー、黄褐色の
❸ a wall with peeling paint: ペンキが剥げかけた壁

「もう質問はありません、ミスター・ダン」

　帰宅した両親をイマニュエルは笑顔で迎えた。彼らは家族として共に夕食を食べたが、イマニュエルはほとんど一言も喋らなかった。食事が済むと、イマニュエルの父親は、面接の結果がどうなろうとお前のことを誇りに思うぞ、ちゃんとネクタイをしていってゆっくり喋るように気をつけるんだぞと言った。「お前なら立派にやれるさ」と父は言った。

　両親が眠ると、イマニュエルはそっとシャワーを浴びた。シャワーから出て、髪に櫛を入れ、おろしたての下着と靴下をはいた。アイロンをかけたタンカラーのスラックスに脚を入れてジッパーを閉めた。茶色い革のベルトを腰の回りに通した。それから白いアンダーシャツを着てエッグシェルブルーのボタンアップを着た。ウィングチップのドレスシューズの紐をきっちり縛った。

　ゆっくり部屋から出て、家から出た。勝手口を極力静かに閉めて、ガレージに入った。アルミ製のバットがペンキの剥げかけた壁に立てかけてあった。イマニュエルはバットをじっと見た。胸のなかのギリギリ、カチッという熱

in his chest hadn't stopped ❶churning since he'd gotten off the bus. It made him feel like the bat would cure everything if he could just grab it and bring it with him to the park. Emmanuel walked toward the bat, then ❷thought better of it. He left his home empty-
5 handed and headed toward Marshall Park.

"Mister Dunn, please ❸recount the night of July the thirteenth."

George Dunn sits on ❹the stand looking ❺sweaty and apolo-getic. Apologetic in an ❻I-sure-am-sorry-❼acting-well-within-my-
10 rights-❽caused-all-this-gosh-darn-hoopla kind of way.

"Well, I was with my two kids—Tiffany and Rodman—when I saw a gang laughing and ❾doing God knows what outside the library."

"Did you ❿at any point ⓫feel threatened, Mister Dunn?"

15 "Well, I didn't at first, but then I realized all five of them were wearing black, like they were about to commit a robbery."

"Are you suggesting that it was these young people's clothes that made them a threat to you and your family?" The prosecution

---

❶ churn(ing): 激しく動く、渦巻く
❷ thought better of it: 考え直してやめた
❸ recount: 〜を詳しく話す
❹ the stand: 証人席
❺ sweaty and apologetic: 汗ばんで、申し訳なさそうな
❻ I-sure-am-sorry: イヤマッタク済イマセンネ
❼ acting-well-within-my-rights: 十分権利ノ範囲内デ行動シタコトガ
❽ caused-all-this-gosh-darn-hoopla: コンナクソ忌々シイ馬鹿騒ギヲ起コシタ。
　 gosh darn は goddamn などよりはいくぶんマイルドな強調句。
❾ doing God knows what: 神のみぞ知ることをやっていた＝何かやってたけど

はバスを降りて以来ずっと渦巻くのをやめていなかった。ただバットを摑んで公園に持っていけさえすれば、バットが何もかもを正してくれるような気がしていた。イマニュエルはバットの方に歩いていったが、思い直した。手ぶらで出かけ、マーシャル・パークに向かった。

「ミスター・ダン、7月13日の夜のことも話してください」

ジョージ・ダンは証言者台に、汗をかいて、申し訳なさげな顔で座っている。いやあほんとに私十分権利の範囲内のことやっただけなのにこんな大騒ぎになっちまってすいませんねえ、というたぐいの申し訳なさ。

「ええ、二人の子供と一緒にいましたら——ティファニーとロドマンです——ごろつきの一団が図書館の外でゲラゲラ笑って、何やってんだかわかんないことをしてるのを見ました」

「いずれかの時点で脅威を感じましたか、ミスター・ダン？」

「ええ、初めは感じませんでしたが、そのうち気がついたんです、五人とも黒い服着て、いまにも強盗とかやりそうだって」

「ということはつまり、この若者たちの服装ゆえに、彼らはあなたとあなたの家族にとって脅威であったということですか？」。検察側はこの瞬間を何

何だったかは全然わからない

❿ at any point: いずれかの時点で

⓫ feel threatened: 脅威を感じる

has been waiting for this moment for weeks.

"No, no. Of course not. It was when one of them, the tall one, ❶started yelling stuff at me. ❷I was afraid for my children—Tiffany and Rodman. That's all I was thinking: Tiffany, Rodman. I had to
5 protect them." ❸Several members of the jury nod thoughtfully.

"And what did Mister Heroy yell at you?"

"I think he wanted my money—or my car. He said, '❹Gimme,' and then something else."

"So at what point did you feel your life was threatened?"

10 " ❺I wasn't about to wait ❻until I saw my life flashing before my eyes. Or Tiffany's or Rodman's. I had to act. I did what I did for them."

"And what did you do?"

"I went and got my ❼saw." Dunn's eyes ❽glow. "I did what I
15 had to do. ❾And you know what—I loved protecting my kids."

The jury stares, attentive, almost ❿breathless. ⓫Engaged and excited.

---

❶ started yelling stuff at me: 俺に向かってギャアギャアわめき出した。stuff は「いろんなこと」。

❷ I was afraid for my children: 子供たちのことが心配だった

❸ Several members of the jury nod thoughtfully: 何人かの陪審員が考え深げに頷く。thoughtfully の一語で、陪審員たちの共感が誰に向けられているかが明らかになる。

❹ Gimme: Give me

❺ I wasn't about to wait: 待つつもりはなかった

❻ until I saw my life flashing before my eyes: 自分の命が目の前で点滅を始める（＝危うくなる）のを見るまで

週間も待っていたのだ。

「いやいや。もちろん違います。そのうちに一人がね、背の高い奴がね、私に向かってギャアギャアわめき出したんです。私、子供たちのことが心配になりまして——ティファニーとロドマンのことが。頭のなかはそれだけでした。ティファニー、ロドマン。私は二人を護らなくちゃいけなかったんです」。陪審員の何人かが考え深げに頷いた。

「それで、ミスター・ヘロイはあなたに向かって、なんとわめいたんですか？」

「金をよこせって言ったんだと思いますね——じゃなきゃ車を、かもしれない。『くれよ』って言って、ほかにも何か言ってましたね」

「それで、どの時点であなたは、自分の命が危険にさらされていると感じたんですか？」

「自分の命が目の前で点滅はじめるまで待つ気はないね。じゃなきゃティファニーやロドマンの命が。ここは行動しなきゃいけない。二人の子供のためを思って、やったんです」

「で、何をなさったんです？」

「ノコギリ、取りに行ったんです」。ダンの目が輝く。「やるべきことをやったんです。それでね——いい気持ちでしたよ、自分の子供を護るのは」

　陪審員たちはじっと注意深く、ほとんど息を止めて見入っている。熱心に、ワクワクした気分で。

❼ (a) saw: のこぎり
❽ glow:（内側から光を発するかのように）輝く
❾ And you know what: それでですね。p. 164, 註❸に同じ。
❿ breathless: 息を殺して、かたずをのんで
⓫ Engaged:（話に）引き込まれて

*

The night was cool. Under an ❶unspectacular sky, Emmanuel felt
the story of the Finkelstein Five on his fingers and in his chest and
in each of his breaths. He imagined George Wilson Dunn ❷walking
5 free down the courtroom steps as cameras flashed. Emmanuel
turned around and went back to his garage where the bat was
waiting for him. It was from his Little League days. He'd played
second base. The bat was too big for him then, too heavy. Now it
was just right. He took it and walked to the park. I'm awake now;
10 Boogie had said something like that while they were on the bus.

  "Looking like a young ❸Hank Aaron, bro," Boogie said as
Emmanuel approached. With Boogie was ❹a middle school
biology teacher Emmanuel remembered as Mr. Coder, as well as a
girl named Tisha, Boogie's girlfriend, and another tiny man with
15 glasses. Mr. Coder and the tiny man each wore three-piece suits,
navy blue and ❺coal black respectively. Their eyes looked cold and
dead. Tisha wore a flowing yellow dress with a ❻festive hat that
had a kind of veil that ❼swooped across the front of it. On her left

---

❶ unspectacular: パッとしない
❷ walking free down the courtroom steps: 自由の身で法廷の階段を降りて
  いく
❸ Hank Aaron: 偉大な黒人ホームランバッター（1934-2021）。
❹ a middle school biology teacher: 中学校の生物の先生。middle school の
  長さは地域によって異なるが、第5または第6学年から第8学年までが多い。
❺ coal black: 石炭のように黒い＝真っ黒な
❻ festive: 華やかな
❼ swooped across the front of it: すうっと前面を覆っていた

＊

　夜は涼しかった。パッとしない空の下、フィンケルスティーン・ファイブの物語を自分の指先に、胸のなかに、息一つひとつのなかにイマニュエルは感じた。ジョージ・ウィルソン・ダンが自由の身で裁判所前の階段をカメラのフラッシュを浴びながら降りていく姿をイマニュエルは想像した。イマニュエルは回れ右して、バットが彼を待つガレージに戻っていった。リトルリーグで使っていたバットだ。彼は二塁を守っていた。そのころバットは彼には大きすぎ、重すぎた。いまはちょうどいい。バットを手にとり、公園まで歩いていった。俺は目覚めた。ブギーもバスに乗ってたときそんなようなことを言っていた。

　「若きハンク・アーロンみたいだぜ」イマニュエルが近づいていくとブギーが言った。ブギーと一緒に、たしかミスター・コーダーという名前の中学校の生物の先生と、ブギーのガールフレンドのティーシャという名前の女の子と、もう一人眼鏡をかけた小男がいた。ミスター・コーダーと小男は三つ揃いのスーツを着ていて、色はそれぞれネイビーブルー、コールブラックだった。彼らの目は冷たく、死んでいるみたいに見えた。ティーシャは流れるような黄色いワンピースを着て、前面をベールみたいなのに覆われた華やかな帽子をかぶっていた。左手には優雅な白い手袋を持っている。ブギーはけさ

hand was an elegant white glove. Boogie was wearing the same white shirt and slim red tie he'd had on that morning. *Gang.* **❶**That was the word they'd use.

"My bro Manny **❷**has the right idea," Boogie said after a quick
5 exchanging of names. "Today we're going all the way. I hope you know how to swing that thing." Boogie **❸**crouched into a stance and **❹**rocked an imaginary bat back and forth like Ken Griffey Jr. Then he **❺**took a hard step into an invisible fastball that he **❻**crushed into the cheap seats. Emmanuel's body **❼**tensed. Boogie laughed
10 and ran around a tiny diamond. "All the way," he said as he **❽**rounded the bases.

"So you've grabbed your chain saw. What happens next?"

"The tall one, he was so tall, he must have been a basketball
15 player or something, he says he's **❾**not scared of no hedge cutter, and he comes charging at me."

"So an unarmed J. D. Heroy **❿**came charging at you while you were holding a chain saw — **⓫**totally unprovoked."

---

❶ That was the word they'd use: 彼ら（世間、白人たち）はその言葉 (gang) を使うだろう

❷ has the right idea: 正しい考えを持っている＝ちゃんとわかっている

❸ crouched into a stance: かがんで（バッティングの）構えに入った

❹ rocked an imaginary bat back and forth like Ken Griffey Jr.: ケン・グリフィー・ジュニアのように架空のバットを前後に揺り動かした。名打者ケン・グリフィー・ジュニア（1969- ）は構えに入って投球を待つときバットを前後に細かく揺り動かすのが癖だった。

❺ took a hard step: ぐいっと踏み込んだ

❻ crushed into the cheap seats: 安い席（外野席）に叩き込んだ

❼ tense(d): 緊張する

と同じワイシャツ、赤のナロータイ。ギャング。世の中は自分たちについて
その言葉を遣うだろう。

「マニーは俺のブラザーなんだ、こいつはちゃんとわかってるんだ」とブギー
は手早く名前の紹介を済ませたあとに言った。「今日はとことん最後までや
る。お前がそいつの振り方、わかってるといいがな」。ブギーはかがんで構え、
架空のバットをケン・グリフィー・ジュニアみたいに前後に振った。それか
ら大きく踏み込み、見えない速球を外野席に叩き込んだ。イマニュエルの体
が緊張した。ブギーが笑いながら小さなダイヤモンドを一周した。「とことん
最後まで」とブギーは言ってベースを回った。

「で、あなたはチェーンソーを摑んだと。次はどうなります？」
「背の高い奴がね、ものすごく高い奴でね、きっとバスケットボールか何か
の選手だったんだね、そんな生垣カッターなんか怖いもんかとか言いながら
ね、私に向かって突進してきたんだ」
「では、武器を携帯していないJ・D・ヘロイが突進してきて、あなたはチェー
ンソーを構えていたと——何の挑発も受けていないのに」

❽ rounded the bases: ベースを（ダイヤモンドを）回った
❾ not scared of no hedge cutter: 生け垣用バリカンなんか怖くない（否定語
　が二つあるのは崩れた英語では普通）
❿ came charging: 突進してきた
⓫ totally unprovoked: 何の挑発も受けずに

"Totally."

"What happened next?"

"**❶***Vroom*, I had my young children, Tiffany and Rodman, behind me **❷**so I could, *vroom, vroom*, protect them."

"What exactly does that mean?"

"That I **❸**revved my saw and **❹**got to cutting."

"You 'got to cutting'? Please, Mister Dunn. Please **❺**be specific."

"*Vroom*. I **❻**cut that basketball player's head clean, *vroom*, off."

"And then what?"

"Then three more of them **❼**rushed me. They tried to **❽**jump me."

"And as these children were running toward you, what did you do? Did you ever think to run? **❾**Get into your truck and go?"

"Well, I checked to see if Tiffany and Rodman were safe, and then I **❿**went to make sure they stayed safe. I was too worried about my kids to think about running."

"And how did you 'make sure they stayed safe,' Mister Dunn?"

---

❶ *Vroom*: エンジン音を表わす擬音語。
❷ so I could ... protect them: 俺が彼らを守ってやれるように
❸ revved my saw: チェーンソーの回転を増した
❹ got to <get to ...: ～に取りかかる
❺ be specific: もっと具体的に言ってください
❻ cut that basketball player's ...: cut ... clean off で「～をきれいに切り落とした」。
❼ rushed me: 襲いかかってきた
❽ jump me: 飛びかかってくる
❾ Get into your truck and go?: Did you ever think to get into ...?
❿ went to make sure ...: しっかり～になるようにしに行った

「そう」

「次はどうなります？」

「ヴルルン、私の幼い子供たちがうしろにいた、ティファニーとロドマンと、俺がヴルルン、ヴルルン、守ってやれるように」

「それ、いったいどういうことです？」

「回転数上げて、切りにかかったってこと」

「『切りにかかった』？　すみません、ミスター・ダン。具体的におっしゃってください」

「ヴルルン。バスケットボール選手の首切ったんだよ、ヴルルン、綺麗にスパッと」

「で、それから？」

「それから、もう三人突進してきた。私に襲いかかってきたんだ」

「で、その子供たちが駆け寄ってきて、あなたは何をしたんです？　逃げよう、と考えたりしましたか？　トラックに乗り込んで逃げようとか？」

「いや、まずティファニーとロドマンが大丈夫か確かめてから、二人がそのあともしっかり大丈夫なように手を打ちに行ったんだ。子供たちのことが心配で、逃げるなんて考えもしなかったね」

「で、『二人がそのあとも大丈夫なように』どういう手を打ったわけですか、ミスター・ダン？」

"I got to cutting." George Dunn pantomimes pulling ❶the rip cord of a chain saw several times.

"You ❷mutilated five children."

"I protected my children."

5

Emmanuel was surprised to see he was the only one of the group who carried a weapon. He felt a strange pride.

"So where are we getting them?" Mr. Coder asked.

"Right here. We'll wait in Tisha's car for a couple to come
10 round trying to use their car as ❸a love box. This is the spot for that," Boogie said. He pinched Tisha's side.

"I want to know who we're Naming," Tisha said, ❹swatting Boogie's hand away playfully. "That matters," she finished, her voice dropping to seriousness.

15

"And what about Fela St. John?" the prosecution asks, finally.

"Which one is that?" George Dunn replies quickly.

The prosecuting attorney smiles, her eyes are bright and

---

❶ the rip cord: チェーンソーを始動させる紐。
❷ mutilate(d): (人の手足などを) 切断する
❸ a love box: セックスをする場所
❹ swat(ting): (ハエなどを) ぴしゃっとはたく

「切りにかかったのさ」。ジョージ・ダンはチェーンソーの紐を引っぱるパントマイムを何度かやってみせた。

「あなたは五人の子供たちを切り刻んだ」

「自分の子供たちを守ったのさ」

　グループのなかで武器を持っているのは自分だけなのを見てイマニュエルは驚いた。妙なプライドを感じた。

「で、どこでやるんだ？」とミスター・コーダーが訊いた。

「ここだよ。ティーシャの車にみんな入って、いちゃつきに来るカップルの車を待つんだ。ここ、そういうスポットなんだよ」とブギーが言った。そしてティーシャの脇腹をつねった。

「誰をネーミングするのか知りたい」とティーシャが、ブギーの手をふざけてはたきながら言った。「それって大事よ」と言い終えた彼女の声は真剣な低さに落ちていた。

「で、フェラ・セントジョンは？」検察官が最後に訊く。

「それってどいつ？」とジョージ・ダンがすかさず返す。

　検察官はにっこり笑い、彼女の目は明るく輝き、少しもひるまない。「7

❶unflinching. "The seven-year-old girl. The cousin of Akua and Marcus Harris. What about the seven-year-old girl you **❷**decapitated with a chain saw?"

"She looked a lot older than seven to me," Dunn replies.

5   "Of course. How old did you think she was as you pulled **❸**the blade through her neck?"

"Maybe thirteen or even fourteen."

"Maybe thirteen or fourteen. And you approached her—you ran after her and murdered her. The reports show you killed her
10 last and that she **❹**was found yards from the rest. Did you have to chase her? How fast was she?"

"She didn't run anywhere. Tried to attack me, same as the rest of them."

"Fela St. John, the seven-year-old girl, tried to attack you, a
15 grown man who she had just watched murder some of her friends and family. And **❺**somehow her body was found in a completely different area. Do you think that **❻**adds up? Does that sound like a seven-year-old girl to you?"

---

❶ unflinching: ひるまない
❷ decapitate(d): 〜の首を切る
❸ the blade: 刃
❹ was found yards from the rest: ほかの子たちから何ヤードも離れたところ
　 で発見された
❺ somehow: なぜか
❻ add(s) up: つじつまが合う

つの女の子ですよ。アクア・ハリスとマーカス・ハリスのいとこ。あなたが
チェーンソーで首を切り落とした 7 つの女の子はどうなんです？」

「私には 7 つよりだいぶ上に見えたけどね」とダンは答える。

「そうでしょうとも。あの子の首に刃を通したとき、いくつだと思いました？」

「13 か、ひょっとして 14 かな」

「13 か 14 かなと。で、あなたはその子に近づいていった。その子を追いか
けていって殺したんですよね。報告によると、その子を殺したのが最後で、
その子だけ何メートルも離れたところで見つかったそうですね。わざわざ追
いかけなくちゃいけなかったんですか？　その子、どのくらい速く走ってた
んです？」

「どこにも走りやしなかったよ。ほかの奴らと同じで、私に襲いかかってき
たんだ」

「フェラ・セントジョン、7 歳の女の子が、あなたに襲いかかってきた、たっ
たいま自分の友だちやきょうだいを殺すのを見た大人の男性であるあなた
に。そしてなぜか彼女の死体は全然違う場所で見つかった。それって筋が通
るとあなた思います？　それって 7 歳の女の子がやることに聞こえます？」

"She looked at least thirteen."

"Does that sound like a thirteen-year-old girl to you, Mister Dunn?"

"These days," Dunn says, "❶you just never know."

5

"Fela," Emmanuel said. "Fela St. John." He could see those news photos of her ❷in her Sunday best: a shining yellow dress and bright ❸barrettes in her hair. Then the pictures that had leaked to the internet: her tiny ❹frame dressed in blood, headless.

10   "Okay. Now we just ❺gotta wait," Boogie said. He started walking toward Tisha's car. The group followed. "When they ❻get going, we're gonna ❼run up on them, ❽crack open a window, and pull 'em out. ❾No playing around. ❿We're doing this right."

They didn't have to wait very long. The couple looked young.
15 Emmanuel only ⓫glimpsed them ⓬for a second as they ⓭turned hard into the parking lot. They parked, and soon their silver ⓮sedan was ⓯bouncing gently. All Emmanuel knew for sure was that one had brown hair and the other blonde.

---

❶ you just never know: わからんものだぜ
❷ in her Sunday best: よそ行きの服を着て
❸ barrette(s): 髪留め、バレッタ
❹ frame: 骨格、体
❺ gotta: got to
❻ get going: やり出す
❼ run up on them: 奴らのところに飛んでいって襲う
❽ crack open a window: 窓を叩き割る
❾ No playing around: ふざけたりはしない（すぐ要件に取りかかる）
❿ We're doing this right: これはきちんとやるんだ

「少なくとも 13 に見えたんだ」

「それって 13 の女の子がやることに聞こえます、ミスター・ダン？」

「近ごろはわからんもんだぜ」とダンは言う。

「フェラ」とイマニュエルが言った。「フェラ・セントジョン」。よそ行きの服を着た彼女の報道写真がイマニュエルの目に浮かんだ。ぴかぴかの黄色いワンピース、髪には明るい色のバレッタ。それから、インターネットに漏れた別の写真——小さな体が血に包まれ、首はない。

「オーケー。あとは待つだけだ」とブギーが言った。そしてティーシャの車の方に歩いていった。みんなもついて行った。「向こうがやり出したら、寄っていって、窓を叩き割って、そいつらを引っぱり出す。ふざけたりしない。こいつはちゃんとやるんだ」

　長く待つ必要はなかった。そのカップルは若く見えた。イマニュエルは車がぐいっと曲がって駐車場に入ってきたときに一瞬見ただけだった。二人は車を駐め、やがてその銀色のセダンがゆるやかに揺れ出した。イマニュエルにはっきりわかるのは、一人が茶色い髪で一人が金髪だということだけだった。

⑪ glimpse(d): 〜をちらっと見る

⑫ for a second: 一秒間、ほんの一瞬

⑬ turned hard: ぐいっと大きく曲がった

⑭ (a) sedan: 箱型の自動車

⑮ bouncing <bounce: 上下に動く、跳ねる

"All right, I want to ❶put it in blood ❷real quick," said Boogie as he pulled a small box cutter from the glove compartment. He handed the cutter to Tisha, who took his right forearm. She brought the blade to his skin and, ❸with surprising ease, cut a
5 large 5 into him. "It feels good, ❹I swear," Boogie said as he ❺bit his lip and looked into ❻the rearview. Once Tisha was finished, she handed the cutter to Boogie, who ❼scooted closer to her and ❽reached over the middle console so he could carve a 5 into Tisha's shoulder. "It's gonna be okay; don't be nervous," Boogie said.
10 Tisha ❾took several sharp breaths in, then ❿exhaled in a great wave once he was finished. Emmanuel could see the 5 ⓫sprout up in red. Boogie turned in his seat to hand Mr. Coder the blade. "⓬Shit, ⓭they look like they might be getting ready to dip, we gotta move." Boogie took his blade back, then looked at Emmanuel. "Hit
15 those windows," Boogie said to Emmanuel, who was sandwiched between the two older men. "Then we'll pull 'em out."

Boogie unlocked and opened his door first, then Tisha opened

---

❶ put it in blood: 血に染める
❷ real quick: すごい早く。日本語の「すごい」が副詞化している（「すごく」の意味で使われるようになっている）のと同じように、real も口語では really の意味で使われる。
❸ with surprising ease: 驚くほど易々と
❹ I swear: ほんとだぜ。何かを断定、断言するときに使う。
❺ bit <bite: ～を噛む
❻ the rearview: バックミラー
❼ scoot(ed): さっと動く
❽ reached over the middle console: 真ん中のコンソールの向こうに手をのばした。console は運転席と助手席のあいだにある小物入れ。

「よし行くぞ、すぐに血を流すんだぞ」とブギーは言いながら、グラブコンパートメントから小さなカッターナイフを出した。カッターをティーシャに渡すと、ティーシャはブギーの右腕の手首近くを摑んだ。そして刃をブギーの肌に当て、驚くほど容易に大きな5を切り込んだ。「いい気持ちだぜ、ほんと」とブギーは唇を嚙んでバックミラーを見ながら言った。ティーシャが作業を終えてカッターをブギーに渡すと、ブギーはすっとティーシャの方に寄って、ティーシャの肩に5を彫ろうと真ん中のコンソール越しに身を乗り出した。「上手く行くよ。ピリピリしなくていい」とブギーは言った。ティーシャは何度かハッと息を吸い込み、ブギーが終えるとふうっと大きな波を吐き出した。5が赤く現われるのがイマニュエルにも見えた。ブギーは体を回してミスター・コーダーにカッターを渡した。「まずい、あいつらそろそろ行きそうだぞ、さっさと動かないと」。ブギーはカッターを取り返し、それからイマニュエルを見た。「あの窓、ぶっ叩くんだ」とブギーは、年上の男二人にはさまれているイマニュエルに言った。「そしたらみんなで引きずり出す」

　ブギーがまず自分の側のロックを外してドアを開け、ティーシャが彼女の

❾ took several sharp breaths in: ハッと何度か強く息を吸った
❿ exhale(d): 息を吐く
⓫ sprout up: パッと出現する
⓬ Shit: まずい、やばい
⓭ they look like they might be getting ready to dip: あいつら、もうじき帰り支度しそうに見える。dip: to leave, depart（*Urban Dictionary*）

hers. The air that ❶flooded into the car ❷felt charged. Emmanuel waited for the two men sitting ❸on either side of him to open their doors. The group of them walked slowly across ❹the lot. ❺The bopping stopped. They knew. *Fela St. John.* He said the name to
5 clear his head. *Fela St. John. Fela St. John.* Emmanuel imagined the fear the couple in the car might be feeling. He imagined each of the Finkelstein Five. Emmanuel ran forward and, ❻with a force he imagined could crush anything, swung his bat into the rear window on the right side. The bat met the glass and ❼clanked.
10 His body was ❽tingling with energy, and where there had been grinding and heat, there was ❾an explosion. "Fela St. John!" he ❿roared, and swung at the window a second time. It ⓫shattered, and suddenly the night ⓬was aflame with screams.

"Oh shit!" a voice from the car screamed. The other screamed
15 in the language of fear. No words.

"Fela St. John," Emmanuel screamed from somewhere deep inside himself. He ran to the other side of the car and smashed the other rear window in three swings. The screams, already

---

❶ flood(ed): (洪水のように) どっと入ってくる
❷ felt charged: 電気が通っているみたいに感じられた
❸ on either side of him: 自分の両側に
❹ the lot: 駐車場 (the parking lot)
❺ The bopping: (カップルの車の) 揺れ
❻ with a force he imagined could crush anything: 何だって叩き壊せると思える力で
❼ clank(ed): ガツンと鳴る
❽ tingling <tingle: 疼く、うずうずする
❾ an explosion: 爆発
❿ roar(ed): 絶叫する

側を開けた。車のなかに流れ込んできた空気は電気を帯びているように思えた。イマニュエルは左右に座った男がそれぞれドアを開けるのを待った。グループはゆっくり駐車場を歩いていった。向こうの車の揺れが止まった。気がついたのだ。**フェラ・セントジョン**。頭をすっきりさせようとイマニュエルはその名を口にした。**フェラ・セントジョン。フェラ・セントジョン。**車のなかのカップルが感じている恐怖をイマニュエルは想像してみた。フィンケルスティーン・ファイブの一人ひとりを想像してみた。イマニュエルは飛び出していき、何でも割れると思える力を込めてバットを振り、右側の後部席の窓に叩きつけた。バットがガラスとぶつかってガツンと鳴った。体じゅうにエネルギーが疼いた。いままでギリギリと熱かったところに、爆発が生じた。「フェラ・セントジョン！」と彼は声を張り上げ、もう一度窓にバットを降りおろした。窓が粉々に割れて、突如夜の空に悲鳴が燃え上がった。「ヤバい！」車の中で一人の声が絶叫した。もうひとつの声は恐怖の言語で絶叫した。言葉はない。

「フェラ・セントジョン」とイマニュエルは、自分のなかのどこか奥深くから絶叫した。車の反対側に駆けていって、そっちの窓も三発で叩き割った。すでにありえないくらい騒々しかった悲鳴が二倍の強さになった。何もかも

⓫ shatter(ed): 粉々になる
⓬ was aflame with screams: 直訳は「悲鳴で燃え上がった」。

❶ impossibly loud, ❷ doubled in intensity. ❸ Everything sounded like everything else. The other door was open, then closed, open, then closed, in ❹ a tug of war between Boogie and the man in the car.

5   "FELA ST. JOHN!" Boogie yelled, pulling the man's ❺ torso and head out of the car. His arm still gripped the door. Boogie raised his foot and kicked hard at the top of his head. Tisha did the same; she wore ❻ wedges that fell on the man's head like bricks. Red blood ❼ drizzled the concrete. After a few more ❽ stomps, he seemed

10 mostly powerless and ❾ let them drag his body out. The man in the glasses and Mr. Coder had the other door open and pulled out the woman, a young girl, maybe in college, who was kicking and yelling sounds that Emmanuel had heard only in horror movies.

15 " ❿ I beg of you, I implore you, ⓫ not to consider anything but the facts," the prosecutor says to begin her closing. "Over the last several days, we've heard the accused try to ⓬ wiggle out of one simple fact: he murdered five children completely unprovoked.

---

❶ impossibly: ありえないほど
❷ doubled in intensity: 激しさが倍になった
❸ Everything sounded like everything else: どの音も声もものすごく大きく、かつ交じりあって区別のつけようのないすさまじさを伝えている。
❹ a tug of war: 綱引き
❺ (a) torso: 胴体
❻ wedges: wedge heels
❼ drizzle(d): 霧雨のように降る。p. 8, l. 1 で名詞として既出。
❽ stomp(s): 踏むこと
❾ let them drag his body out: 体を彼らに引きずり出させた＝引きずり出され

がほかの何もかもと同じような音になった。もうひとつのドアが開き、閉まり、開き、閉まり、と、ブギーと車中の男とのあいだで綱引きがくり広げられた。

「フェラ・セントジョン！」とブギーがわめき、男の胴と頭を車から引っぱり出した。男の片腕はまだドアにしがみついていた。ブギーは片足を上げて、男の頭を思いきり蹴った。ティーシャも同じことをやった。ウェッジヒールを履いていて、それが煉瓦のように男の頭に落ちていった。赤い血がコンクリートにたらたら垂れた。さらに何度か踏まれた男は、ほとんど力が抜けたように見え、体を引きずり出されても抵抗しなかった。眼鏡の男とミスター・コーダーはもうひとつのドアを開けて女を、まだ若い娘を、大学生だろうか、を引っぱり出し、女は足をばたばたさせて暴れ、イマニュエルがホラー映画でしか聞いたことのない音を叫んでいた。

「皆さんにお願いします、どうかお願いします、ひたすら事実だけを検討してください」と検察官は言って締めくくりにかかる。「この数日間、私たちは被告がひとつの単純な事実から逃れようとするのを聞いてきました。すなわち彼は、何の威嚇も受けずに五人の子供を殺したのです。本人は自分の

ても抵抗しなかった
❿ I beg of you, I implore you: お願いです、どうかお願いします
⓫ not to consider anything but the facts: 事実以外何も考えないよう＝ひたすら事実を検討するよう
⓬ wiggle out of ...: 〜から逃れ出る

He may think his chain saw some holy weapon or a ❶scepter ❷bestowed on him by God, but don't let him ❸go on believing that. Please don't let the blood of these five children— ❹with all the potential in the world— ❺spill into nothingness. Please show
5 us that they mattered. These children who were killed before they ever got a chance to know the world, to love, to hate, to laugh, to cry, to see all the things that we've seen, and finally decide ❻what kinds of people they might want to be. They mattered. Don't let their deaths ❼go unpunished.

10   "We have a system that, though it can never ❽ease the pain, tries to ❾right the wrongs. We have a system that, though it won't ever succeed, attempts ❿valiantly to fill ⓫this all-consuming void ⓬torn into the heart of the world by men like George Wilson Dunn. I happen to be one of the people who are perhaps foolish enough
15 to believe there is a difference between good and evil. Somehow. Still. Please show me I'm not a fool. Show the parents of these children they aren't fools for ⓭demanding justice. ⓮For knowing the idea of justice was born for them and this very moment. Mister

---

❶ scepter: (王の) 笏
❷ bestowed on him by God: 神から授かった
❸ go on believing: 信じつづける
❹ with all the potential in the world: あらゆる可能性を抱えていた、人生すべてこれからだった
❺ spill into nothingness: (血が) 無の中へ流れていく＝まったく無駄に流れる
❻ what kinds of people they might want to be: 自分がどういう人間になりたいか
❼ go unpunished: 罰せられないまま終わる
❽ ease the pain: 痛みを和らげる

チェーンソーを、神から賜った聖なる武器か笏だと思っているかもしれませんが、そんなことを信じたままにさせてはいけません。どうかこの五人の子供の血が、未来のあらゆる可能性を抱えていた五人の子供の血が、無駄に流れたことにしないでください。五人は大切な人間だったことをどうか私たちに示してください。彼らは世界を知るチャンスもないうちに殺されました。愛して憎んで笑って泣いて私たちが見てきたいろんなことを見た末に自分はどんな人間になりたいか、決めるチャンスもないうちに殺されました。彼らは大切な人間でした。その死をもたらしたものが罰を受けぬままに終わらせないでください。

　私たちには、それで痛みが和らぐわけでは決してありませんが、為された悪を正そうと努めるシステムがあります。ジョージ・ウィルソン・ダンのような人間によって世界の中心に狂暴に押し込まれた、すべてを喰らいつくすこの空虚を、果敢に埋めようと努めるシステムが私たちにはあります、その目標が完全に達成されることはないでしょうが。私はたまたま、善と悪のあいだには違いがあると信じる、おそらくは愚かな人間の一人です。なぜか、いまも、そう信じています。どうか私が愚かではないことを示してください。この子供たちの両親に、彼らが正義を求めるのは愚かではないと示してあげてください。正義という観念が、彼らのため、まさにいまこの瞬間のために生まれたのだと知るのは愚かではないと示してあげてください。ミスター・

---

❾ right the wrongs: 不正を正す

❿ valiantly: 果敢にも

⓫ this all-consuming void: このすべてを焼き尽くしてしまう虚無

⓬ torn into the heart of the world: 直訳は「裂かれるようにして世界の中心に押し込まれた」。

⓭ demand(ing) justice: 正義を要求する

⓮ For knowing the idea of justice was born for them and this very moment: 正義という観念が彼らのため、まさにこの瞬間のために生まれたことを知っているからといって。文頭の For は前文の for demanding justice の for と同じ。

George Dunn destroyed something. Maybe the only sacred thing. Show him it matters. Show him that you know these children, Tyler Mboya, Fela St. John, Akua Harris, Marcus Harris, and J. D. Heroy were humans with a heart, just like any one of you."

5

The two white bodies ❶huddled together, ❷trapped in a circle of Emmanuel and the rest of them. The man was crying. His face was ❸bruised. Red flowed from his nose to his lips. ❹He'd been bargaining for the last minute.

10   "Please, please! What can we give you?" His body shook. "Please, it's yours. Please!" The woman huddled on the ground beside him made ❺raspy, choking sounds.

     "Fela, Fela, Fela." It was ❻a trance. Emmanuel tried to look at the eyes of the young couple. He smashed his bat against the
15 concrete several times while yelling the name. The bat ❼bouncing off the ground ❽sang a metallic yelp and ❾shocked electricity into his veins.

---

❶ huddled together: 体を丸めて身を寄せあった

❷ trap(ped): ～を閉じ込める

❸ bruise(d): ～に打撲傷を与える

❹ He'd been bargaining for the last minute: この一分、取引きを企てていた

❺ raspy, choking sounds: 耳障りな、息が詰まったような音

❻ a trance: 恍惚、トランス状態

❼ bouncing off the ground: 地面に当たって跳ねて

❽ sang a metallic yelp: 直訳は「金属的なわめき声を歌った」。金属バットを駐車場のコンクリートに思いきり叩きつけて立つ音を想像していただきたい。

ジョージ・ダンは何かを壊しました。もしかしたら唯一神聖であるものを壊しました。壊したものが意味あるものだと彼に示してください。これらの子供たち、タイラー・ムボイヤ、フェラ・セントジョン、アクア・ハリス、マーカス・ハリス、J・D・ヘロイがあなたたちの誰とも同じく心を持つ人間だったことをあなた方が知っていると、どうかミスター・ジョージ・ダンに示してください」

　二つの白い体が一緒に縮こまって、イマニュエルたちが作る輪のなかに閉じ込められている。男は泣いていた。顔に打ち傷があった。赤いものが鼻から口に流れていた。この一分間、彼は交渉を試みていた。
「頼む、頼むよ！　何をあげたらいい？」。体が震えた。「頼む、なんでもあげる。頼む！」。女は男のかたわらの地面にうずくまって、キーキー耳障りな、息が詰まったみたいな音を立てている。
「フェラ、フェラ、フェラ」。トランス状態だった。イマニュエルは若いカップルの日を見ようとした。バットを何度かコンクリートに叩きつけながらその名をわめいていた。バットは地面に当たって跳ね返ってくるとともに金属的な叫びをあげ、イマニュエルの血管に電気を送り込んだ。

❾ shocked electricity into his veins: 彼の血管の中に電気ショックを送り込んだ

"Say it for me," Emmanuel said suddenly. A ❶screeching, crazy voice came from ❷a part of him he was just discovering, ❸but which he understood had been growing for a very long time. "Say her name," Emmanuel said. He ❹pointed his bat at the couple. "Say
5 her name for me. I need to hear it." He raised his bat, and both the white bodies ❺flinched in response. He ❻crashed the bat down. He felt ❼the bark of the bat against the concrete. *This is what it is to be the wolf*, the bat screamed. *You have been the sheep, but now you are the wolf.* "SAY IT FOR ME. I BEG OF YOU," Emmanuel screamed.
10 This, he knew, was going all the way. He could ❽feel the group feed on his fury. "Fela St. John, Fela St. John, Fela St. John," they chanted in praise. "Tell me you love her," Emmanuel said. "Tell me I'm crazy. I'm begging you. Say her name." Emmanuel looked down at the tears and the red ❾that seemed to be all that was left
15 of the couple. They weren't even people. Just ❿pumping hearts, hormones. He wondered if his rage would end; he imagined it ⓫leaking out of him.

He ⓬figured that at the other side of the tunnel—after the

---

❶ screech(ing): 金切り声を上げる
❷ a part of him he was just discovering: 自分の中の、たったいま発見しつつある部分
❸ but which he understood had been growing for a very long time: だがもうずっと前から育ってきたことがわかる
❹ pointed his bat at the couple: バットをカップルに向けた
❺ flinch(ed): 縮み上がる
❻ crashed the bat down: バットを叩きつけた
❼ the bark of the bat: バットの吠え声
❽ feel the group feed on his fury: 彼の憤怒をグループが糧にしているのを感

「言ってくれ」とイマニュエルは突然言った。甲高い、狂った声が、自分のなかの、たったいま発見しつつある部分、だがもうずっと前から育っていたとわかる部分から出てきた。「あの子の名前、言え」とイマニュエルは言った。そしてバットをカップルに突きつけた。「あの子の名前、言ってくれ。どうしても聞きたいんだ」。彼がバットを持ち上げると、白い体はどちらもびくっと縮み上がった。彼はバットを降りおろして叩きつけた。バットの表面がコンクリートに当たって吠えるのが感じられた。**狼になるってのはこういうことなんだよ**、とバットは絶叫していた。**お前はいままで羊だったけど、いまは狼だ**。「言ってくれ。**お願いだから言ってくれ**」とイマニュエルが絶叫した。最後まで行くってのはこういうことなんだ、とわかった。自分のこの憤怒をグループが吸収しているのが感じられた。「フェラ・セントジョン。フェラ・セントジョン、フェラ・セントジョン」と彼らは讃えて言った。「あの子を愛してるって言ってくれ」とイマニュエルは言った。「俺は狂ってるって言ってくれ。お願いだ。あの子の名前を言ってくれ」。イマニュエルがカップルを見下ろすと、二人とももはや涙と血しか残っていないみたいだった。もう人間でさえない。ただの脈打つ心臓、ホルモン、それだけ。この怒り、いずれ終わるだろうかとイマニュエルは考えた。怒りが自分から漏れ出ていく感じを想像してみた。

トンネルの向こうに行けば、ネーミングが済めば、いい気持ちになるかも

じる
❾ that seemed to be all that was left of the couple: 直訳は「このカップルで残っているすべてであるように思える」
❿ pumping hearts: ポンプのように動く心臓
⓫ leaking out of him: 自分の中から漏れ出ている
⓬ figure(d): 考える、思う

Naming—he might be happy. But as he ❶thrashed and yelled and saw it all, he felt nothing leaving him. There was only throbbing. Yelling and screaming and banging a bat on the ground, he thought that maybe ❷he was being exactly who he really was for
5 once. ❸Doing exactly what was expected of him. The screaming of the couple there, the honesty of their fear—he felt it giving him wings.

Boogie, standing beside Emmanuel, ❹motioned for him to hand the bat over ❺so he could finish what they'd started. Emmanuel
10 looked toward the weeping man. His shirt ❻was on backward. The woman ❼was quieting down. She did not have much more breath to give. But in the middle of all those sounds of rage, ❽timidly but definitely, Emmanuel heard something come from the woman's mouth.

15 "Fela St. John," the woman said. And as she did, Emmanuel looked into the eyes of the woman, and she looked back into his.

"Let me get that," Boogie screamed, opening his palms to receive the bat. "I want to be the one. I want to feel it. Please let

---

❶ thrash(ed): 打ちかかる
❷ he was being exactly who he really was: 自分がいまこそ本当の自分になっているると
❸ Doing exactly what was expected of him: まさに自分に期待されていることをやっていると
❹ motioned for him to hand the bat over: バットをよこすよう彼（イマニュエル）に合図した
❺ so he could finish ...: 〜を彼（ブギー）が終えられるように
❻ was on backward: 前後ろが逆になっていた
❼ was quieting down: 静かになってきていた
❽ timidly but definitely: おずおずと、だがはっきりと

しれない、そう思った。だが叩きつけ、わめき、すべてを見ながら、自分の
なかから何も出ていってはいないことをイマニュエルは感じた。ズキズキと
疼くだけだった。わめき、絶叫し、バットをコンクリートに叩きつけながら、
いま初めて自分が本当の自分になっているかもしれないと思った。まさしく
自分に求められていることをやっている気がした。そこにいるカップルの悲
鳴、彼らの恐怖の正直さ——それが自分に翼を与えてくれるのをイマニュエ
ルは感じた。

　かたわらに立ったブギーが、ケリをつけようと、バットをよこせとイマニュ
エルに合図した。イマニュエルはしくしく泣いている男の方を見た。シャツ
が背中に回っていた。女は静かになってきていた。もうあまり、出せる息も
残っていなかった。けれども、憤怒の音が響きわたるなかで、おずおずと、
だがはっきり、何かが女の口から出てくるのをイマニュエルは聞いた。
「フェラ・セントジョン」と女は言った。女がそう言ったとき、イマニュエ
ルは女の目を見て、女も彼の目を見返した。
「それ、よこせ」とブギーがわめいて、バットを受けとろうと手のひらを開
いた。「俺がキメたいんだ。この手で感じたい。やらせてくれよ。なあったら」。

me. Please." When Emmanuel did not hand the bat over, ❶Boogie's fire blazed brighter. "❷This can't wait. I need this now," he said as he pulled out the box cutter. "I'll start it," Boogie said, looking at Emmanuel.

5   Emmanuel gripped the bat. Boogie's eyes were large and heavy as he turned toward the couple. The blade in his fist grew as his thumb pushed at the box cutter. He stepped forward.

"I don't know what to do!" Emmanuel screamed, and swung the bat full force, cutting the wind in half and hitting Boogie in ❸the
10 flank, crashing the bat at his ❹ribs. The box cutter fell to the floor.

"Ladies and gentlemen. Gentlemen and ladies." The defense stands, ❺strides toward the ❻jurors, ❼adjusts the knot of his tie then continues, "The prosecution has tried to prove that George
15 Dunn is a monster incapable of love. A monster that would ❽hack down five helpless children. But what the prosecution has failed to do is prove that he was not a hero saving his children from five monsters. That may sound ❾harsh, but let's be honest. We've

❶ Boogie's fire blazed brighter: 直訳は「ブギーの炎はより明るく燃え上がった」。
❷ This can't wait: これ以上延ばせない
❸ the flank: 横腹
❹ rib(s): 肋骨
❺ stride(s): 大またに歩く
❻ juror(s): 陪審員
❼ adjust(s): ～を整える
❽ hack down ...: ～をメッタ切りにする
❾ harsh: 厳しい、むごい

イマニュエルがバットを渡さずにいると、ブギーの炎がますます明るく燃えた。「ぐずぐずしてられないんだぞ。いま要るんだよ、それ」と彼は言いながらカッターを出した。「じゃ、俺が始めるからな」とブギーはイマニュエルを見ながら言った。

　イマニュエルはバットを握った。カップルの方を向き直るブギーの目は大きく、重たげだった。こぶしで握ったカッターの刃が、親指でレバーを押すとともにすっと長くなった。ブギーが前に出た。

「わからない、どうしたらいいか！」とイマニュエルは絶叫し、バットを力一杯振って風を二つに切り、ブギーの横腹を打ち、ブギーの肋骨を砕いた。カッターが地面に落ちた。

「紳士淑女の皆さん。淑女紳士の皆さん」。弁護人が立ち上がって、陪審員たちの方に歩いていき、ネクタイの結び目を整えてから言う。「検察官はジョージ・ダンが愛する能力を持たない怪物だと証明しようと試みました。五人の無力な子供をメッタ切りにするような怪物だと。ですがその検察官も、ジョージ・ダンが自分の子供たちを五人の怪物から救った英雄ではないと証明することはできませんでした。酷な言い方かもしれませんが、ここは

seen this story before. A hardworking middle-class white man is put in a situation where he has to defend himself. And all of a sudden he's **❶**a 'racist.' All of a sudden he's a 'murderer.' No motive, no **❷**prior history, except for several ridiculous stories

5 **❸**concocted by **❹**so-called 'childhood friends' and so-called 'family members.' **❺**It's all very convenient, I think. That all these facts and **❻**testimonies suddenly **❼**align perfectly to **❽**incriminate a man who was spending an evening with his children. Before you make your decision, I want you to remember a single word: freedom. It

10 sounds better than prison or death or fear, doesn't it? Freedom just **❾**has a certain ring to it, doesn't it? Bring freedom. Please, please freedom."

Boogie fell to the ground **❿**in a heap. "**⓫**Goddamn it," he screamed.

15 Breathing seemed to be hard for him. Tisha yelled, then **⓬**crawled to Boogie's side on the ground. Her yellow dress **⓭**puddled around her. Boogie mumbled violent words as he **⓮**writhed **⓯**in the middle of a small sun in Tisha's arms. Mr. Coder and the man in glasses

---

❶ a 'racist': 「人種差別をする人間」
❷ prior history: 前科
❸ concoct(ed): 〜をでっち上げる
❹ so-called: いわゆる。その呼び名が事実ではないという含み。
❺ It's all very convenient, I think: まあ実に都合がいいのでしょう（皮肉）。
❻ testimonies <testimony: 証言
❼ align perfectly: ぴったり一列に並ぶ
❽ incriminate: 〜を有罪にする
❾ has a certain ring to it: ある種の響きがある
❿ in a heap: どさっと

正直になりましょう。こういう筋書きを、私たちはこれまでにも見てきました。働き者の、中流階級の白人男性が、自分を弁護せねばならない破目になる。そして突然彼は『人種差別主義者』になるのです。突然『人殺し』になるのです。動機もなく、前科もなく、あるのはいわゆる『子供のころの友人』やいわゆる『家族の一員』がでっち上げた馬鹿馬鹿しいお話だけ。こういうのはさぞ便利なのだろうと思います。そうやって出てくる事実やら証言やらが突如ぴったりつながって、自分の子供たちと一緒に晩を過ごしていた男が犯罪者に仕立て上げられるのです。決定を下される前に、どうか皆さん、ひとつの言葉を思い出していただきたい。『自由』という言葉です。監獄とか、死とか、恐怖とかいった言葉よりよく聞こえるでしょう？　自由という言葉には独特の響きがあるでしょう？　自由をもたらしてください。どうか、どうか自由を」

　ブギーはどさっと地面に倒れ込む。「何なんだ」と絶叫する。呼吸するのも辛そうだ。ティーシャが悲鳴を上げ、ブギーの許に這ってゆく。黄色いドレスが彼女の周りで池を作っている。ブギーはティーシャの腕のなか、小さな太陽に埋もれて身悶えしながら暴力的な言葉をもごもご吐き出す。ミスター・コーダーと眼鏡の男は動きもせず立っている。白人のカップルはいま

⓫ Goddamn it: 何なんだ、何てこった
⓬ crawl(ed): 這う
⓭ puddle(d): 水たまりのように広がる
⓮ writhe(d): もだえる
⓯ in the middle of a small sun: 広がった黄色いドレスが太陽のように見えるというイメージ。

stood without moving. The white couple was now completely silent.

Emmanuel took two steps, dragging the bat on the ground. He stood above the couple. "Fela St. John, Fela St. John!" the couple
5 screamed. Emmanuel looked down on them and saw himself in their eyes. He was the wolf. He felt the bat in his hands. He wanted to stand there forever. He wanted to scream and feel all their fear in his stomach till he burst.

Emmanuel looked around. He heard the screams of police
10 vehicles more clearly now. Mr. Coder and the other man were running away. He heard the sirens, and for the first time in his life, Emmanuel did not fear them.

"Put your hands in the air," a giant voice, one from an entirely different world, said. Emmanuel smiled. He very slowly raised
15 both of his arms. Tisha cried quietly over Boogie, who was still mumbling in a dream.

"Drop the weapon," the voice called. Red and blue lights ❶tie-dyed it all.

---

❶ tie-dye(d): 〜を絞り染めにする

やまったく静かになっている。

イマニュエルは二歩動き、バットを地面に引きずっていった。カップルを見下ろして立った。「フェラ・セントジョン！　フェラ・セントジョン！」とカップルが絶叫した。イマニュエルは二人を見下ろし、彼らの目のなかに自分自身を見た。狼だった。両手に握ったバットを感じた。永久にそこに立っていたかった。精一杯声を張り上げて、自分の胃のなかにたまった彼らの恐怖を、体が破裂してしまうまで感じたかった。

イマニュエルはあたりを見回した。パトカーのサイレンがさっきよりはっきり聞こえてきた。ミスター・コーダーともう一人の男が逃げ出した。サイレンが聞こえて、生まれて初めてイマニュエルはサイレンが怖くなかった。「両手を上に上げろ」と巨大な声が、全然違う世界からの声が言った。イマニュエルはにっこり笑った。すごくゆっくり両腕を上げていった。ティーシャはブギーの上にかがみ込んで静かに泣き、ブギーはまだ夢のなかでもごもご呟いていた。

「武器を捨てろ」と声が呼びかけた。赤と青の光がすべてを絞り染めにした。

"Fela St.—" Emmanuel began as he dropped the bat with his hands held above his head. He thought of the names. Then he felt it. The feeling of his Blackness rising to an ❶almighty 10.0. He heard ❷a boom that was like the child of thunder. He saw his own
5 brain ❸burst ahead of him. ❹Hardy red confetti. His blood splashed all over the pavement and the couple. He saw the Finkelstein Five dancing around him: Tyler Mboya, Akua Harris, J. D. Heroy, Marcus Harris, Fela St. John. They told him they loved him, still, forever. In that moment, with his final thoughts, his last feelings
10 as a member of the world, Emmanuel felt his Blackness ❺slide and plummet to an absolute ❻nothing point nothing.

15

❶ almighty: 全能の
❷ a boom: (銃などの) 轟き
❸ burst: 破裂する
❹ Hardy red confetti: 直訳は「頑丈な赤い紙吹雪」。
❺ slide and plummet: 滑り、急降下する
❻ nothing point nothing: 0.0

「フェラ・セント──」両手を頭の上に上げバットを捨てながらイマニュエルは言いはじめた。五つの名前のことを考えた。と、それが感じられた。自分の黒人度が、全能の 10.0 まで上がるのが。雷の子供みたいなバン！という音が聞こえた。自分の脳味噌が目の前で破裂するのが見えた。がっしり重い、赤い紙吹雪。自分の血が舗道とカップルの上に飛び散った。フィンケルスティーン・ファイブが自分の周りで踊るのをイマニュエルは見た。タイラー・ムボイヤ、アクア・ハリス、J・D・ヘロイ、マーカス・ハリス、フェラ・セントジョン。五人は彼に言っていた、あんたのこと愛してるよ、いまも、いつまでも。その瞬間、最後の思いを抱え、世界の一員としての最後の感情を抱えて、イマニュエルは自分の黒人度が一気に落ちていき、まったくの 0.0 になるのを感じた。

ちなみに

　この「ザ・フィンケルスティーン5」は、作者と同じくガーナ系の
黒人青年を主人公とし、黒人としてアメリカで生きることから生じる
恐怖と怒りを描いているところは作者の体験が反映しているだろう
が、もうひとつ、作品の大きな源となっているのは、トレイヴォン・
マーティン射殺事件である。2012年2月26日、フロリダ州サンフォー
ドで、武器も持っていなかった17才の黒人少年を、自警団員の男性
が射殺し、裁判となって無罪になった事件である。これに対して挙がっ
た抗議の声が「ブラック・ライヴズ・マター」運動に発展した。ちな
みにアジェイ゠ブレニヤーは、別短篇では、コミュニティの安全を脅
かす侵入者を撃ち殺す快感に浸れるテーマパークを辛辣に描いている
("Zimmerland")。

授業後の雑談

　6篇精読、お疲れさまでした。自分と価値観の違う「他者」とどうかかわるか、自分は他者をどう見ているか、といった事柄は、今日小説を考える上でつねに大きな問題です。まあそもそもどんな小説であれ、読むこと自体「他人になってみる」ことだと言えるのかもしれませんが。ここで取り上げた6篇が、そういうことを考えるきっかけになれば幸いです。以下、雑談的補足です。

　Stuart Dybek, "Farwell" を冒頭に収めた *The Coast of Chicago* は、同じ登場人物がくり返し現われるというわけではありませんが、何と言ってもシカゴ（の主として下町）という舞台は共通しているし、また、〈超短篇↔短篇のくり返し〉という構成もあって、明らかに作品間につながりが感じられ、いわゆる短篇集（a collection of stories）というより連作短篇集（a novel-in-stories）という性格が強い一冊です。人と同じくらい「場所」も主人公だという意味で、James Joyce, *Dubliners*（1914）や Sherwood Anderson, *Winesberg, Ohio*（1919）などの古典的名作とも通じるものがあります。

　この "Farwell" もそうですが、ダイベックは小説を通して音楽を喚起する手腕が見事です。"Chopin in Winter"（*The Coast of Chicago* 所収）のショパンとブギウギ、"A Minor Mood"（*I Sailed with Magellan* 所収——これも *The Coast of Chiago* 以上にスケールの大きい見事な連作短篇集です）の "You Are My

Sunshine" やジーン・クルーパのドラムス……。この「英文精読教室」シリーズの続篇を出せるなら、いずれ「文章から音楽を聴く」という巻も作りたいですが、そのときはかならずやダイベック氏に再登場してもらうことになるでしょう。

Paul Bowles はこの "You Are Not I" のほかにも、タンジールをはじめとする異国の地を舞台に他者との強烈な（多くの場合暴力的な）遭遇を描いた強烈な短篇をいくつも書いていて、それらは *The Stories of Paul Bowles*（2006）にひととおり収められています。

僕がこの "You Are Not I" を初めて読んだのは、*Double/Double*（1987）という非常に面白い分身譚アンソロジー（Michael Richardson 編、Penguin Books, 1987）を手にしたときでした。ポーやホフマンの有名な分身譚をすべて外し、いわばそういう定番分身譚の分身（double）として編まれたこのアンソロジーで、ボウルズや Eric McCormack に出遭い、しかも訳すことまでできたのは大きな幸運でした。*Double/Double*、長らく絶版で少し入手しづらいかもしれませんが、abebooks.com（古本を探すのに最適のサイトです）で見るとまだ手ごろな値で買えるようです。

"A Vision" の著者 Rebecca Brown に初めて会ったとき、自分はレズビアン作家として知られるけれどレズビアンの主人公が成功・勝利するような物語は書かないからレズビアンの読者にはあまり読まれないし、それ以外の読者にはレズビアンだからということでやはりあまり読まれない、と、決して愚痴っぽくなく乾いた口調で語っていました（もちろん、そういう線引きとは関係なしに彼女の作品を愛読する読者は、アメリカのみならず

日本にも大勢います）。この "A Vision" は比較的珍しく、自分のレズビアンとしての目覚めを、一種宗教的覚醒のように書いていて、広い意味での「勝利」の物語と言えるかもしれません。実際この作品は、*A Woman Like That: Lesbian and Bisexual Writers Tell Their Coming Out Stories*（Joan Larkin 編、Avon, 1999）というアンソロジーが初出で、ほかのレズビアン・バイセクシャル作家の作品が並ぶ中にすんなり溶け込んでいます。

　日本語が母語で、少しでも英語を教えた経験のある人なら、Linh Dinh, "!" を読んで、身につまされる瞬間がまったくない、ということはまずないでしょう。もちろんディンはこの短篇で、ひとつの文化が他文化を支配したり、より強力な他文化に崇拝と憎悪の両面感情を抱いたりする事態を戯画的に描いているのであり、自分は本当の英語を教えていないんじゃないか、という日本人教師のうしろめたさを念頭に置いているわけではないのですが、まあ時にはそんなふうに、自分に引きつけて小説を読んでも作者は許してくれると思います（それにもちろん、日本で英語を教えるという行為の背後にも、文化と文化の力関係が隠れていると考えることは可能でしょうし）。

　この "The Dysfunctional Family" に限らず、Agnes Owens が遺した短篇・中篇が素晴らしいのは、スコットランドの労働階級の人々の、良くてパッとしない、悪ければ悲惨な状況を描いていても、それを実にシンプルな文章で淡々と描き、感傷をいっさい排して、そこにある種のユーモアさえ生じさせていることです。これがアメリカだと、同じような悲惨を描いても、どうしても「アメリカの夢の裏切り」といった思いが荷物としてついて来

てしまうんですが、オーエンズの文章にはそういう余分な荷物がいっさいありません。*The Complete Short Stories* の、とりわけ最後の *The Dark Side* と題したセクションは（まあほかのセクションだって bright じゃないんですが）、本書的に言うと難易度 1 の、短いなかで強い印象を残す短篇が並んでいます。あいにくペーパーバックは絶版のようですが、Kindle 版があります。

　Nana Kwame Adjei-Brenyah, "The Finkelstein 5" が収められたデビュー短篇集 *Friday Black* は、"The Finkelstein 5" のように現実の黒人少年射殺事件に材をとったものもあれば、著者のアパレル業界でのバイト体験を活かして、はじめから死体置き場が用意してある超人気バーゲンの話などもあったりして、漫画的な荒唐無稽さと、現代アメリカに黒人として生きることの辛さの胸をえぐる実感とが絡みあって見事です。

　ちなみに "The Finkelstein 5" と並んで、2019 年のほぼ同時期に出会って僕が衝撃を受けたもう 1 本の短篇もやはりアフリカ系アメリカ人による作品で、John Keene, "Rivers"（2016）といい、*Adventures of Huckleberry Finn* の逃亡奴隷ジムが語る後日譚です。『ハック・フィン』のなかの、多くの訳者が「おら」と訳してきたジムの口調とはうって変わった、張りつめた語りを通して、「『ハック・フィン』は孤児の少年と逃亡奴隷との友情の物語である」ときれいにまとめて済むものではないかもしれない、ということを考えさせてくれます。難易度は 3+ ですが、ウェブでも読めますから興味のある人は見てみてください。https://www.vice.com/en/article/wd4w39/vice-exclusive-john-keenes-huck-finn-inspired-short-story-rivers-1884

21世紀の射殺事件も、ずっと名作と呼ばれてきた作品のなかの黒人の描かれ方も、等しく強力な作品の素材となる。その背後に広がる歴史を考えると、自分の呑気さが恥ずかしくなりますが、少なくともこれらの作品に、精一杯の敬意をもって接しようという気は僕にもあります。

2021年3月

柴田　元幸

編訳註者

柴田元幸（しばた もとゆき）

翻訳家、東京大学名誉教授。東京都生まれ。ポール・オースター、レベッカ・ブラウン、スティーヴン・ミルハウザー、スチュアート・ダイベック、スティーヴ・エリクソンなど、現代アメリカ文学を数多く翻訳。2010 年、トマス・ピンチョン『メイスン＆ディクスン』（新潮社）で日本翻訳文化賞を受賞。翻訳に、『ハックルベリー・フィンの冒けん』（研究社）、『トム・ソーヤーの冒険』（新潮文庫）、ジョゼフ・コンラッド『ロード・ジム』（河出文庫）、エリック・マコーマック『雲』（東京創元社）、スティーヴン・ミルハウザー『ホーム・ラン』（白水社）など多数。編訳書に、『「ハックルベリー・フィンの冒けん」をめぐる冒けん』、レアード・ハント『英文創作教室 Writing Your Own Stories』（研究社）など。文芸誌『MONKEY』、および英語文芸誌 MONKEY 責任編集。2017 年、早稲田大学坪内逍遙大賞を受賞。

編集協力

滝野沢友理・高橋由香理・田辺恭子・平野久美・青木比登美

組版・レイアウト

古正佳緒里・山本太平

社内協力

三谷裕・望月羔子・高見沢紀子・三島知子・鈴木美和・松本千晶・星野龍

英文精読教室
えいぶんせいどくきょうしつ

第 2 巻
だい かん

他人になってみる
た にん

● 2021 年 4 月 30 日　初版発行 ●

● 編訳註者 ●

柴田元幸
しば た もとゆき

Copyright © 2021 by Motoyuki Shibata

発行者　●　吉田尚志

発行所　●　株式会社　研究社

〒 102-8152　東京都千代田区富士見 2-11-3

電話　営業 03-3288-7777 （代）　編集 03-3288-7711 （代）

振替　00150-9-26710

http://www.kenkyusha.co.jp/

KENKYUSHA

装丁　●　久保和正

組版・レイアウト　●　渾天堂

印刷所　●　研究社印刷株式会社

ISBN 978-4-327-09902-2 C1082　Printed in Japan

柴田元幸〔編・訳・註〕 英文精読教室 全6巻

第1巻 物語を楽しむ

- 英語で書かれた最良の小説を精選し、読者が一人で隅々まで
  味わえるよう、詳細な註と解説を施した全6巻シリーズ。
- 読者が自分の読みを確認できるよう、対訳も付す。
- 各巻ごとにテーマを決めて、好みの内容が選べるよう配慮。
  古典から現代まで幅広く、英語圏全体から作品を選択。また
  作品ごとに難易度を表記。

A5判 並製 258頁
ISBN 978-4-327-09901-5 C1082

目 次

シリーズの構成

〈既刊〉
- 第1巻 物語を楽しむ
- 第2巻 他人になってみる

〈続刊予定〉
- 第3巻 口語を聴く
- 第4巻 性差を考える
- 第5巻 怪奇に浸る
- 第6巻 ユーモアを味わう

編訳註者より

　外国語を短時間読んで、一定の情報を解析し、処理するような読み方が、グローバル化したと言われている今の世の中ではたぶん要請されているのだと思います。それはそれで大事なことにちがいありません。でもそういう、脳内ストップウォッチと競争するような読み方からちょっと離れて、英語で書かれたすぐれた小説をゆっくりじっくり読みたいと思う人もそれなりにいるにちがいない、そしてそういう人たちの多くは、その助けになるような本があったらいいのにと思っているにちがいない……そうした確信からこのシリーズは生まれました。

　翻訳で読んでも、もちろん小説のよさは、かなりの部分、感じとれます。ですが、原文をじかに読んで味わえる楽しさは、やはり格別です（翻訳者が言うんだから間違いありません）。そして、楽しむために必要なのは、語学力です。また逆に、語学力をつけるのに最良の手段は、楽しんで読むことです。語学的なことをあれこれ考えながら、小説の中で生きている人たちのこともあれこれ考えているうちに、語学力も小説を楽しむ力も自然と身につくような、そういう体験をこのシリーズが提供することを願って、知恵を絞って作品を選び、註をつける。要するに、「自分が学生のころにあったら使ったと思える本」を作りました。同好の士が集まってくれますように。